Total Quality
Customer Service

Total Quality
Customer Service

How To Make
It Your Way Of Life

by Jim Temme

SkillPath Publications
Mission, KS

Editor: Kelly Scanlon

Cover Design: Rod Hankins

Page Layout: Theresa Morgan, Dave McCullagh, Rod Hankins

ISBN: 1-878542-44-3

Temme, Jim, 1946-
    Total quality customer service : how to make it your way of life / by Jim Temme
        p.   cm.
    Includes bibliographical references.
    ISBN 1-878542-44-3 :
    1. Customer service. I. Title.
HF5415.5.T46 1994
658.8'12—dc20   94-2719
                                                                      CIP

        4   5   6   7   8   9   10   06   05   04

Printed in the United States of America

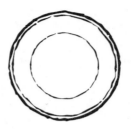

Contents

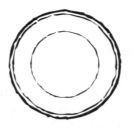

Introduction

*Customer service is a way of life,
not a promotional campaign.*

This is a book about getting beyond the banners, the buttons, and the contest drawings that are so often promoted in the name of "customer service." It is a book filled with practical, "hands-on" techniques for living out customer service everyday. Because after all is said and done—long after the balloons have deflated, the buttons have been tossed in a drawer, and the banners have found sanctuary on some backroom shelf—showing a genuine commitment to customer service, to follow-through and caring, is the only way to earn the loyalty that keeps customers coming back week after week, month after month, year after year.

Everyone in the organization—from management to front-line employees must be committed to providing quality customer service. Management, in particular, must set the tone for continuous improvement of goods and services, procedures, and employees in order to meet customer needs, whether the organization is for-profit, nonprofit, or government.

This book is divided into fourteen chapters that cover such topics as customer service leadership, training, achieving customer service excellence, re-engineering, teamwork, marketing and selling, handling customer complaints, dealing with difficult customers, communication skills, and telephone etiquette. The topics are intentionally diverse because customer service is about so many things. It goes well beyond the traditional view of serving external customers (those who seek your goods and services) efficiently. It starts on the inside—with you. If internal customers (employees) treat one another with dignity and with respect, then they are likely to treat external customers in the same way.

In the often-quoted words of Ralph Waldo Emerson, "Who you are speaks so loudly I can't hear what you're saying."

In other words, *customer service is not just a promotional campaign; it is a way of life!*

As you read through the book, you will be asked to evaluate your own customer service situations and to complete exercises designed to reinforce the concepts that are presented.

By the time you have completed this book, you should be able to answer these questions:

- What am I (or my company) doing to continually seek out customer needs?
- What am I (or my company) doing to continually enhance the quality of goods and services?
- What are the differences between cost-driven and customer-driven companies?

- What is the impact of poor employee training and how do I go about getting the training I need?
- How do I create a customer-oriented environment?
- What goals can I (or my company) work toward to become more effective at providing quality customer service?
- What are the characteristics of a successful customer service team?
- What service level do I operate at, and what are the traits of the customers at that level?
- What do I offer my customers in terms of value?
- How do I create a managed perception (image) that tells my customers they are receiving value?
- Why do my customers complain?
- How well do I handle difficult customers?
- How well do I communicate with and listen to my customers?
- In what areas can I improve my telephone skills?

Finally, don't file this book away on a shelf when you have completed it. Reread it and redo the exercises about every six months. Remember, achieving quality customer service is an ongoing process that requires commitment. In other words:

Customer service is a way of life, not a promotional campaign!

Understanding What
Customer Service
Is Really All About

"*Look at our balance sheet. On the asset side you can still see so-and-so many aircraft with so-and-so many billions. But it's wrong; we are fooling ourselves. What we should put on the asset side is last year SAS carried so-and-so many happy passengers. Because that's the only asset we've got—people who are happy with our service and are willing to come back and pay for it once again.*"

Jan Carlzon
Scandinavian Airlines and author of
Moments of Truth

Customer service is a way of life, not a promotional campaign.

Have you ever entered a bank, a grocery store, a hotel, or any other business where people were wearing name tags and where banners on the wall proclaimed the customer to be Number One—and then you waited in line for twenty minutes to be served? Then when it was finally your turn, the person behind the counter looked at you and said, "Yeah, what d'ya want?" If so, then you know what it's like to be exposed to a promotional campaign that pays more attention to *lip* service than to *customer* service.

There is nothing wrong with a promotional campaign—if the people wearing the buttons live up to the values they say they believe in. If they announce that customers are Number One, then they had better treat customers like they are! In other words, the company—from management to front-line employees—must "walk the talk." Their actions must reflect their words.

All too often, though, the words can be hollow. There is no sincere attempt to really serve customers. Unfortunately, some business leaders believe that if they hire an advertising agency to develop a promotional campaign, customers will flock to them to purchase their goods and services. What they may not understand is that such superficial attempts at customer service do not buy the one important thing today's customers are loyal to: *value.*

What is value? It is a combination of *quality* and *price.* Customers want the highest quality they can get at the best price. Quality means excellent customer service, quality goods and services, and efficient procedures and follow-through.

Defining Customer Service

Broken down, this is the definition of customer service:

- *Customer service* is meeting the needs of the customer.
- A *customer,* or *client,* is anyone who uses goods and services.
- *Service* is any incident of doing for others for a fee or exchange.

What makes one effective at meeting customer needs? Consider these differences between a customer service "superstar" and a customer service "superdud."

A customer service SUPERSTAR is:
- Knowledgeable.
- Self-confident.
- Energetic.
- Timely.
- A good listener.
- Quality-oriented.
- An effective communicator.
- A team player.
- Patient.

A customer service SUPERDUD:
- Is rude.
- Is angry.
- Has a bad attitude.
- Is unwilling to help.
- Frequently interrupts.
- Needs to be the center of attention.
- Wants to work alone or with things rather than with people.

Add others:

_____

_____

_____

_____

_____

_____

_____

Add others:

_____

_____

_____

_____

_____

_____

_____

The Customer Service Flowchart

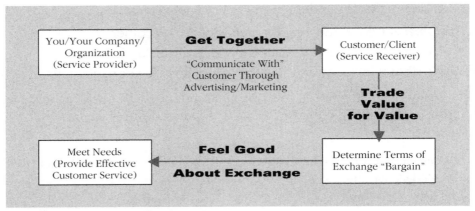

Figure 1. A customer service flowchart.

Meeting customer needs is a step-by-step process (see Fig. 1):

1. Your company or organization is in business to provide a product or service; therefore, you are a *service provider*.

2. You and your company *communicate* to customers the features and benefits of your goods and services through marketing and advertising.

3. Potential and past customers call you *to have their needs met*. They believe or want to determine that your product or service can help them. Customers are *service receivers*.

4. Trading value for value means customers perceive your product or service to be helpful or of value to them. They, in turn, are willing to give up something of value to get your product or service, usually their money or time. Thus, they are trading *value for value*.

5. The *terms of exchange* are what your customers must give up in order to receive the product or service.

6. If the goods or services meet your customers' needs, your customers feel good about the exchange. If you are caring and meet their needs, they are pleased.

Here are six basic principles to adhere to when determining your customers' needs:

1. Determine what your customers *really* need and want. Don't make assumptions about their needs.
2. Concentrate on *quality* in making the product or service available.
3. *Define* how you will get the product to your customer most efficiently or make the service readily available.
4. Provide *leadership* and a culture that is truly service-oriented.
5. Hire good people and *train* and *retrain* them.
6. Continually *survey* your customers to determine whether you are really meeting their needs.

Peter Drucker, the management scholar, defines quality in a product or service as "not what the supplier puts in. It is what the customers get out and are willing to pay for. Customers only pay for what is of use to them and gives them value. Nothing else constitutes quality."

> ▶ The Marriott Hotel chain initiated a fifteen-minute delivery guarantee for breakfast in 1985. Marriott's breakfast business, the biggest portion of the company's room-service revenue, jumped 25 percent. Marriott continues to encourage its employees to devise better ways to deliver meals on time, including having deliverers carry walkie-talkies so they can receive instructions more quickly.

Assessing Your Response to Customer Needs

1. List below what you are doing to continually seek out customer needs.

_____

_____

_____

_____

_____

_____

_____

_____

_____

2. List below what you are doing to continually enhance the quality of your products and services.

_____

_____

_____

_____

_____

_____

_____

_____

_____

Customer vs. Employee Perspective

With all the day-to-day work you have to do, you can easily lose sight of the way your customers see you and your company. Be careful not to let that happen. Sometimes you may wrongly assume that your customer sees you in the same way that you see yourself. Figure 2 illustrates how perspective may differ between the employees of a company and the company's clients.

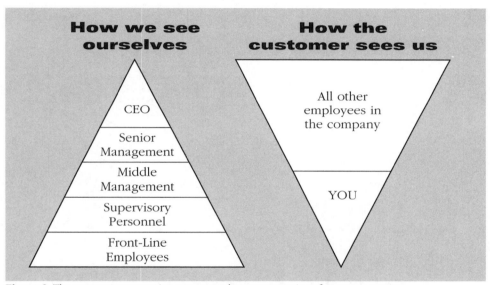

Figure 2. The customer perspective versus employee perspective of customer service.

During any transaction or exchange with a customer, your perspective may be that numerous employees are available to serve that customer and meet his or her needs. During the transaction, however, the customer is speaking to only *one* person. That person is *you*. The customer is not acquainted with all the other people in your company. That customer has a need to be met, and you are the person expected to meet it. To that customer, YOU ARE THE COMPANY!

In his book *Moments of Truth*, Jan Carlzon explains that every moment that you come into contact with a customer is called a moment of truth. What you want to create are *positive* moments of truth.

2

Setting the Tone for
Excellent
Customer Service

▬

*"Management has to set a tone and then constantly
push, push, push."*

Thomas Pritzker
Hyatt Hotel Chain

Management's Role in Creating a Customer Service Culture

Upper management in any organization plays a major role in determining what the company values. If the leadership truly believes in excellent customer service, that is what the company, through its employees, will live up to each day.

It is not enough just to talk about outstanding customer service. It is how management demonstrates its importance and sets the tone for it that determines whether a company's culture is truly customer-driven. In other words, management must *walk its talk.*

Setting the tone means truly valuing excellence in customer service— treating *customers* and *internal customers* (employees) with dignity and respect and meeting their needs.

Consider the following story from *At America's Service,* by Karl Albrecht:

> Abraham Lincoln had a favorite riddle he liked to spring on people. He would ask, "How many legs does a dog have, if you call the tail a leg?" When the unsuspecting respondent would answer "five," Lincoln would chastise: "No, he has four. Calling his tail a leg doesn't make it a leg."

And calling mediocre service "excellent" doesn't make it excellent.

Here are come key points customer service leaders must consider to create a customer-driven culture:

- **Research** ▶ *Continually survey customers—internal and external—to determine needs.* Learn how you can improve your products and services, and determine how the company perceives itself in terms of the quality of customer service it provides.

- **Mission** ▶ *Define the company's mission.* A clearly defined mission truly reflects the company's values. Communicate that mission to internal and external customers. Be sure the mission statement is up-to-date and accurately reflects customer needs.

- **Values** ▶ A company's values are directly related to its mission. *Every day live out values that reflect a customer-driven culture.* The more consistently you follow these values, the greater chance that employees will believe in the values and reflect them day after day.

- **Training** ▶ Real leaders know that their most important asset is their people. Remember, *employees are the company.* Effective leaders realize that one of their major roles in customer service is to be sure that employees receive basic training and continual updates.

How can management get internal customers to be responsive to its efforts to create a customer service culture?

If you care about your employees (internal customers), they are more likely to care about the customers who are interested in your goods and services. Employees don't care how much you *know* until they know how much you *care.*

Consider this: The Nordstrom family is known for setting the tone for outstanding customer service at its Seattle-based department stores. Nordstrom employees will go so far as to iron a new shirt for a customer who is about to attend a meeting, deliver clothes and shoes to shut-ins, and complete special alterations in a timely fashion. Every sales representative (not salesclerk) keeps a profile of repeat customers, calls them about new items, and writes thank-you notes after the sale. Does this kind of service just happen? No—the Nordstrom family sets the tone. Because Nordstrom values internal customers (employees), they in turn value the external customer. In fact, the Nordstrom "employee manual" consists of only one page (Fig. 3), but in that one page is this clear, simple message: We're glad you're a part of the team, and we have confidence in you.

Remember, the leadership in the organization sets the tone for excellent customer service. Consider that:

- Bill Marriott writes thank-you letters to his hotels' frequent guests.
- Embassy Suites' most important criterion for new managers is being able to treat every employee as competent.

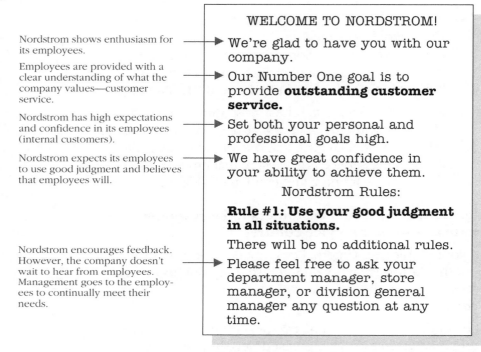

Nordstrom shows enthusiasm for its employees.

Employees are provided with a clear understanding of what the company values—customer service.

Nordstrom has high expectations and confidence in its employees (internal customers).

Nordstrom expects its employees to use good judgment and believes that employees will.

Nordstrom encourages feedback. However, the company doesn't wait to hear from employees. Management goes to the employees to continually meet their needs.

WELCOME TO NORDSTROM!

We're glad to have you with our company.

Our Number One goal is to provide **outstanding customer service.**

Set both your personal and professional goals high.

We have great confidence in your ability to achieve them.

Nordstrom Rules:

Rule #1: Use your good judgment in all situations.

There will be no additional rules.

Please feel free to ask your department manager, store manager, or division general manager any question at any time.

Figure 3. Sample of Nordstrom's company handbook.

- At least half the managers at Marriott and Guest Quarters have been promoted from customer service positions.
- From the president on down, Avis executives staff counters or service cars for several weeks each year. By working hands-on with customers, company leaders don't lose sight of customer service goals.

The Role of the Employee in Setting the Tone

It is not just the responsibility of management to create an excellent customer-service-oriented company or organization. Each employee, or internal customer, has key roles to play. Not only must the company meet the needs of the employee through ongoing training and education, the employee must focus on the company's needs. It is a part of the exchange in trading value for value.

Here are some of the employee's key roles in assisting the company:

- **Give feedback.** ▶ Communicate frequently with management about your needs—training, resources, comfort level, and goals and direction. Also, provide advice on how to improve procedures, products, and services.

- **Show commitment.** ▶ In return for your paycheck and security, it is important to be committed to the company's mission and goals and to your co-workers. This is another example of trading value for value—you give commitment and you receive a salary and security.

- **Adhere to company values.** ▶ Values are the principles that you should bring to work each day—honesty, follow-through, sincerity, trustworthiness, responsibility, dedication to quality, a courteous and friendly attitude.

- **Learn and be focused.** ▶ You have an obligation to learn about your company's (and, therefore, *your*) products and to be able to communicate their features and benefits to customers. You must be focused—to keep your mind on your job and to look for ways to continuously improve yourself and your products and services.

Job Values

What are some of *your* job values?

_____

_____

_____

_____

_____

_____

_____

A Customer-Driven Culture vs. a Cost-Driven Culture

To stay in business for the long run, you must create a company culture that is customer-driven. In *Customers for Life,* Joan Cannie says that 80 percent of customer problems are caused by management policies that are cost-driven rather than customer-driven. Most companies that have initiated customer-driven service have found that the return on the investment averages 10 to 1.

Consider the differences between a company that is cost-driven and one that is customer-driven.

Here are the actions of cost-driven companies:

1. Cut back on service
2. Reduce the number of employees during tough times (the opposite of what should be done)
3. Reduce employee training
4. Decrease quality (a huge mistake)
5. Cut back on the resources needed to serve customers efficiently

Determining the Actions of Cost-Driven Companies

What else do cost-driven companies sometimes do?

_____

_____

_____

_____

_____

_____

_____

Here are the actions of customer-driven companies:

1. Give value-added service (service beyond what is expected)

   Example:

   A young executive traveling on an airline mentioned to the flight attendant that he was excited to get home because it was his wedding anniversary. As the plane approached the airport, the flight attendant brought the man a bottle of champagne, iced down in a shoe box. She didn't have to do that. It was an act of kindness—a value-added service that the executive still remembers.

2. Train and retrain employees
3. Always concentrate on quality
4. Do everything possible to get needed resources
5. Offer special incentives to external and internal customers to show you care
6. Increase the ambience in your place of business
7. Add phone lines, if needed, so that customers won't hear busy signals when they call

4

Determining the Actions of Customer-Driven Companies

What else do customer-driven businesses do?

_____

_____

_____

_____

_____

_____

_____

Focus of Attention

- **Customers** ✔
- **Timeliness** ✔
- **Training** ✔
- **Follow-through** ✔
- **Knowledge** ✔
- **Quality** ✔

Staying Focused On Customer Service Activities

So often management and employees can get bogged down in the minutiae—too many meetings, too many reports (for them and their customers), too many rules and restrictions, too much rhetoric and not enough action. They lose sight of what is important. Constantly ask yourself whether you are working on the right activities—those that will give you and your customers the greatest payoff.

Here are several high-payoff customer service activities:

- **Maintain a service-based culture.** Customer service leadership means, in part, that everyone in the organization needs to take responsibility to care for and nurture customers—both internal and external. Regular maintenance prevents problems. (It's like checking the oil in your car and adding it, if necessary, so your car won't explode.)

- **Declare war on bureaucracy**. Too often, employees and staff are asked to complete too many reports, attend too many meetings, and document decisions at too many levels, which becomes cumbersome to the point that the customer is no longer the focus. Employee efforts should be directed toward meeting customer needs. To do that, they have to be out where the customer is—communicating, listening, and following through. Meeting customer needs is a high-payoff activity.

- **Continually seek ways to enhance the quality of your goods and services.** In today's marketplace, educated consumers want quality. Price, too, is a consideration in for-profit companies. They have to be competitive. What customers really want is value for whatever they give up—time, money, or expertise. It is necessary to constantly consider how you can improve quality in your products and services, in your procedures, in your employee training programs, in communicating effectively, and in delivering and following through on your customer service promises.

- **Advertise.** You can have the best product or service in the world, but if nobody knows about it, you won't be in business very long. Consider how much you can spend to advertise, who you are trying to reach, and the best medium for reaching that audience.

CHAPTER 3

Getting the **Training** *You Need*

"For years we did not have a way to reinforce the training. We were training people at the counter to be nice, to smile, to say the right things, to handle complaints efficiently. But it fell off because the managers weren't filling in. They weren't saying that customer service was an important part of the job."

Director of Training
Budget Rent-A-Car

What Can You Do to Get More Training?

Don't assume that you'll automatically receive all the training you'll need to turn in a top-notch performance or even an adequate one.

Consider this college student's first job experience:

Mark was working in a grocery store as a stocker. Now stocking shelves seemed a simple enough task to Mark, but he received no training for his job. He didn't know the rules or the standards—how many shelves he should be able to stock in an hour, for example. He relied on other stockers to educate him about the proper placement of items and how to create attractive displays. Although management did not spend much time formally training Mark, he thought he was doing a good job of educating himself.

After three weeks, the store manager asked to see Mark in his office. Mark thought, "Oh boy, maybe I'm getting a raise."

Instead, the manager told Mark that he was being put on probation because he was too slow. He said that Mark needed to improve drastically within the next two weeks or he'd be fired. Although Mark was eager to perform up to standards, or even beyond, he still didn't know what the store considered good performance. Only after he asked did he get the direction he needed.

What's the point of the story? Management has an obligation to provide direction and training to every employee at every level, in every position. But equally important, as an employee, you have an obligation to speak up and ask for the training you need to perform well. If you don't, management often assumes that you understand the job and their expectations. Then, when things aren't all right, you may be blamed.

Considering the Impact of Poor Training

Think of a job for which you weren't properly trained. What were some of the drawbacks you encountered in serving customers as a result of your lack of training?

_____

_____

_____

_____

_____

_____

_____

_____

_____

Here's how to get the training you need:

1. **_Seek it out._** Although asking for training does not guarantee you will receive it, you can be reasonably sure you _won't_ get training if you don't ask.

2. **_Be focused._** Learn by doing. Truly concentrate on your job so that you can learn when you do something well or make a mistake. Being focused means being committed to your work. Remember: The key difference between a job and a career is commitment.

3. **_Keep notes in a workbook._** Write down what you learn and what you do well. Doing so gives you a greater chance of grasping practices and procedures that can benefit you and others. For instance, if you are learning a new phone system, write down the procedures in your notebook to help you remember them. Your notes will also serve as a reference if you become confused.

4. ***Become an expert.*** Tell yourself that you want to be an expert about some part of your job. Becoming an expert requires commitment and self-study. It also means putting in more than forty hours a week. The payoff is two-fold: You will feel good about yourself and your customers will feel good about you.

5. ***If you're not getting the training you need, keep asking.*** Be persistent. Continually seek out knowledge. It will make all the difference in how customers perceive you.

Remember: Lack of training can reflect on you negatively. It's difficult to serve customers and meet their needs if you don't know what to do.

Focusing on Your Training Needs

Think seriously about the areas where you need training in order to serve customers more efficiently. Then check them off the list in Exercise 6.

Areas Where I Need Training

- [ ] More information about the company's basic procedures
- [ ] Background about who our customers are and what they look like (their demographics)
- [ ] More information about the features and benefits of our goods and services
- [ ] Basic communication skills (presentation, listening, and written)
- [ ] Policy and procedures for returned goods and unsatisfactory services
- [ ] How to handle customer conflict, including how to control my own emotions when dealing with difficult, upset, or angry customers
- [ ] How to use the phone system efficiently

| | Basic assistance with computers

| | Assistance with the following software package(s):

_____

_____

| | Direction on how to complete the following company report(s):

_____

_____

| | How to sell ideas, products, and services:

_____

_____

| | Other areas where I could use assistance:

_____

_____

Asking for Training: What to Say and How to Say It

Now that you've identified the areas where you'd like to receive some training and direction, ask your supervisor for help.

If you go to your supervisor and say "I need more training," or worse yet, "You need to give me more training," your request will likely be denied. The first approach is not specific and the second one sounds like you're making a demand. How do you approach the subject without being taken too lightly, on the one hand, or putting your supervisor on the defensive, on the other?

Here's how:

• *Use "I" statements.* Using them allows you to speak assertively without putting the person to whom you're speaking on the defensive.

- *Avoid "you" statements.* They sound demanding and accusatory.

  Example:

  "How can you expect me to do this job if you don't train me? You need to explain it to me further."

- *Be specific* about what kind of training you need and about the time and place for the training so that you can serve your customers well.

  Example:

  "I really need more training on the commands for the new pricing and specifications software package. It would be most helpful if I could have the training no later than this Friday. I could schedule some time for training between 3:00 and 4:00 tomorrow afternoon. How can I get your help?"

- *Be sincere in your voice tone.* Show that you sincerely want to become a more knowledgeable and efficient employee.

A word to supervisors:

Frequently observe your employees and ask them questions about the direction and assistance they need. In the book *In Search of Excellence: Lessons From America's Best-Run Companies,* Tom Peters and Robert Waterman, Jr., refer to such behavior as MBWA—Management by Walking Around. The sooner you can correct mistakes, solve problems, and teach employees what they need to know, the more efficiently you can serve customers.

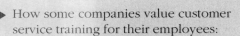

How some companies value customer service training for their employees:

- Kentucky Fried Chicken's new employees must learn 29 basic skills.
- At Embassy Suites, new employees must learn the hotel's basic jobs.
- At Guest Quarters, new staff receive 20 to 40 hours of basic training.

Achieving **Customer** *Service Excellence*

"Success is never final."

J.W. Marriott, Sr.

Getting to Excellence—Creating a Customer-Oriented Climate

Many companies continue to be *cost-driven* rather than *customer-driven*. Their emphasis is on cutting back—cutting services, people, and quality.

Certainly, prudence is necessary to manage resources and to stay in business. However, customer service excellence—being *truly customer-driven*—can set a company apart from its competition. For some executives and companies, becoming customer-driven will take a *transformation*. That is, the company will need to change the basic way it conducts business.

What changes does your company need to make to transform its climate into one that is customer-oriented? You might consider calling your work team together to creatively brainstorm about the changes your department or company could make to serve customers with excellence. During this brainstorming session, assume that you could do anything you want, that any or all of your suggestions would receive management approval. Then begin to find ways to make the suggested changes a reality.

Here are some examples of how other companies changed their operating procedures to serve customers better:

- Customers of General Electric said there was no convenient way to store wine in the refrigerators the company made. So GE added wine racks to its top-of-the-line models.

- Many buyers of one popcorn manufacturer complained that the popcorn was too salty, so the company added a salt-free version to its line. Other companies followed suit.

- Callers on Pillsbury's toll-free line kept asking for copies of a Bundt cake recipe that had appeared in one of the company's ads. There was such interest that Pillsbury formulated a Bundt cake mix and successfully added it to the company's product line.

Source: *Business Week,* March 12, 1990

Transforming Your Company to a Customer-Oriented Climate

1. Brainstorm several ways to transform your company climate into one that is customer-oriented.

_____

_____

_____

_____

_____

_____

_____

_____

2. Choose at least one of the suggestions and devise a way to implement it.

_____

_____

_____

_____

_____

_____

_____

_____

_____

_____

Follow-Through and Caring: What If You Don't Have Both?

As mentioned several times throughout this book, management sets the tone for creating a customer-driven culture. In doing so, equal attention must be given to follow-through and caring. Everyone in the organization must deliver goods and services both on time and consistently, with a minimum of mistakes. Caring and nurturing of the customer must be evident in every transaction.

What happens when there isn't a balance between follow-through and caring? You don't achieve customer service excellence.

Consider figures 4 to 6 that follow.

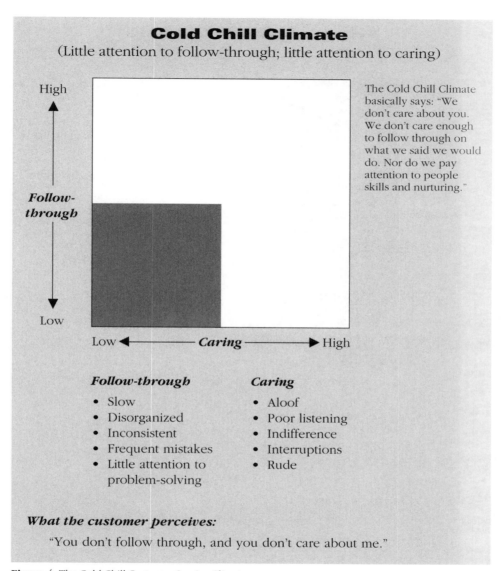

Cold Chill Climate

(Little attention to follow-through; little attention to caring)

The Cold Chill Climate basically says: "We don't care about you. We don't care enough to follow through on what we said we would do. Nor do we pay attention to people skills and nurturing."

Follow-through
- Slow
- Disorganized
- Inconsistent
- Frequent mistakes
- Little attention to problem-solving

Caring
- Aloof
- Poor listening
- Indifference
- Interruptions
- Rude

What the customer perceives:

"You don't follow through, and you don't care about me."

Figure 4. The Cold Chill Customer Service Climate.

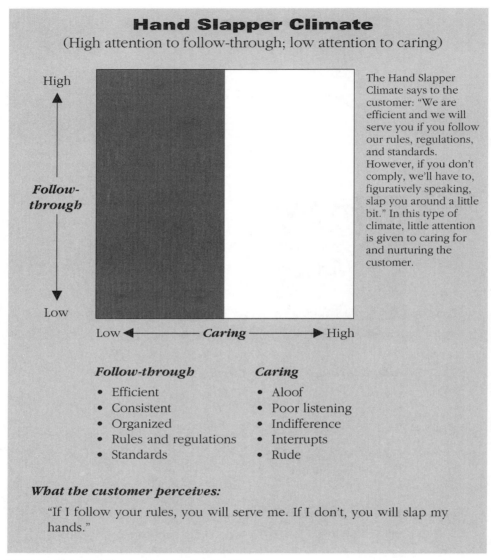

Hand Slapper Climate
(High attention to follow-through; low attention to caring)

The Hand Slapper Climate says to the customer: "We are efficient and we will serve you if you follow our rules, regulations, and standards. However, if you don't comply, we'll have to, figuratively speaking, slap you around a little bit." In this type of climate, little attention is given to caring for and nurturing the customer.

Follow-through
- Efficient
- Consistent
- Organized
- Rules and regulations
- Standards

Caring
- Aloof
- Poor listening
- Indifference
- Interrupts
- Rude

What the customer perceives:

"If I follow your rules, you will serve me. If I don't, you will slap my hands."

Figure 5. The Hand Slapper Customer Service Climate.

Back Slapper Climate

(Low attention to follow-through; high attention to caring)

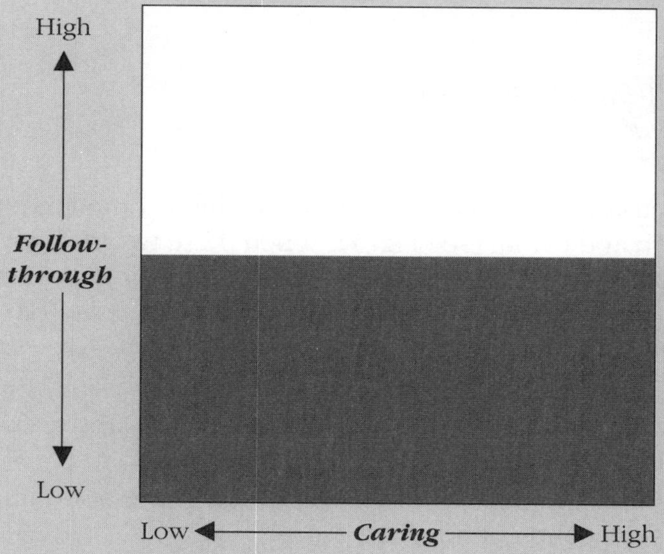

High

Follow-through

Low

Low ◄——— **Caring** ———► High

The Back Slapper Climate says to the customer: "We put on a 'good show.' We smile a lot; we slap you on the back and want to be your friend, but our procedures and follow-through are disorganized and slow. We make the same mistakes over and over. We really don't know what we're doing." There is little attention to follow-through, even though the organization acts as though it cares.

Follow-through

- Slow
- Disorganized
- Inconsistent
- Frequent mistakes
- Little attention to problem-solving

Caring

- Empathic
- Oriented toward meeting needs
- Listens to customer concerns
- Provides "value-added" service
- Makes customers feel important

What the customer perceives:

"You seem to care and listen, but you don't follow through, and you really don't know what you're doing."

Figure 6. The Back Slapper Customer Service Climate.

What Is Quality In Customer Service?

Quality in everything we do and everything we are!!!

Achieving quality in customer service means having a high commitment to both follow-through and caring (see Fig. 7). When these two details are carried out company-wide, the company is well on its way to achieving customer service excellence. Research from the Forum Corporation substantiates this. Consider the five dimensions of service quality reported in the study:

1. ***Reliability.*** Is what was promised provided dependably and accurately?
2. ***Assurance.*** Are the employees knowledgeable and courteous, and can they express trust and confidence?
3. ***Empathy.*** Are caring and individual attention provided?
4. ***Responsiveness.*** Is there a willingness to help customers and to provide prompt service?
5. ***Tangibles.*** Are the physical facilities and equipment customer-friendly? For example, if two dry cleaners you are considering are equal in their services and quality, you may choose the one with the cleanest windows.

Source: Eric R. Blume, "Customer Service: Giving Companies the Competitive Edge," *Training and Development Journal* (Sept. 1988).

▶ *"We can rise from the ashes like a phoenix, but it will take a transformation to do it."*

W. Edwards Deming

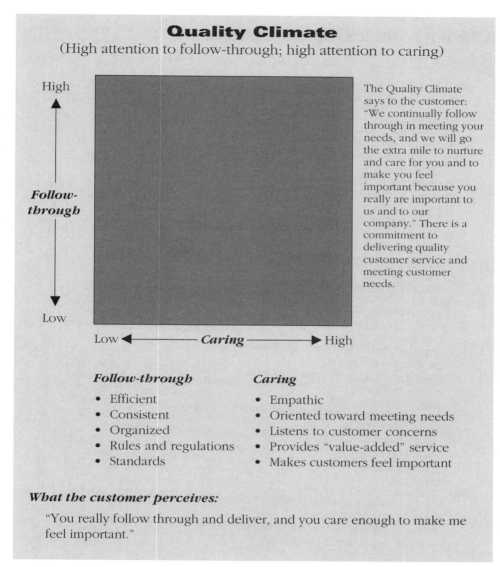

Quality Climate
(High attention to follow-through; high attention to caring)

High

Follow-through

Low

Low ◄——— *Caring* ———► High

The Quality Climate says to the customer: "We continually follow through in meeting your needs, and we will go the extra mile to nurture and care for you and to make you feel important because you really are important to us and to our company." There is a commitment to delivering quality customer service and meeting customer needs.

Follow-through	*Caring*
• Efficient	• Empathic
• Consistent	• Oriented toward meeting needs
• Organized	• Listens to customer concerns
• Rules and regulations	• Provides "value-added" service
• Standards	• Makes customers feel important

What the customer perceives:

"You really follow through and deliver, and you care enough to make me feel important."

Figure 7. The Quality Customer Service Climate.

A Letter From a Satisfied Customer

My husband and I bought one souvenir the last time we were in Tokyo—a Sony compact disc player. The transaction took seven minutes at the Odakyu Department Store.

My in-laws, who were our hosts in the outlying city of Sagamihara, were eager to see their son's purchase, so he opened the box for them the next morning. But when we tried to demonstrate the player, it wouldn't work. We peered inside. It had no innards!

My husband used the time until the Odakyu store would open at 10:00 a.m. to practice for the rare opportunity in that country to "wax indignant." But at a minute to 10, he was preempted by the store ringing us.

My mother-in-law took the call. Odakyu's vice president was on his way over with a new disc player.

A taxi pulled up 50 minutes later and spilled out the vice president and a junior employee, who was laden with packages and a clipboard. In the entrance hall, the two men bowed vigorously.

The younger man read from a log that recorded the progress of the store's efforts to rectify its mistake, beginning at 4:32 p.m. the day before, when the salesclerk alerted the store's security guards to stop my husband at the door.

When that didn't work, the clerk turned to his supervisor, who turned to his supervisor, until a "SWAT Team" leading all the way to the vice president was in place to work on the only clues—a name and an American Express card number. Remembering that the customer had asked him about using the disc player in the U.S., the clerk called 32 hotels in and around Tokyo to ask if a Mr. Kitwasei was registered.

When that turned up nothing, the Odakyu clerk commandeered a staff member to stay until 9:00 p.m. to call American Express headquarters in New York. American Express gave him our New York telephone number. It was after 11:00 p.m. when he reached my parents, who were staying at our apartment. My mother gave him my in-laws' telephone number.

The younger man looked up from his clipboard. He gave us, in addition to the new $280 disc player, a set of towels, a box of cakes, and a Chopin disc.

Source: *Communications Briefings*, November 1990

CHAPTER

5

Setting
Customer
Service Goals

---

*"One of the most important things an organization
can do is determine exactly what business it is in."*

Peter Drucker
Service America

Being Goal-Oriented to Improve Products, Services, and Procedures

One basic question you must consider is this:

If your company, department, or team did not have goals, what would you work on?

Your response: _____

_____

_____

Did you list any of these responses?

1. Whatever comes before you
2. Whatever is easiest
3. Whatever gets your immediate attention
4. Whatever you want to work on

If your company operates without goals, it probably spends much of its time in crisis management. Why? Because if there are no customer-oriented, customer-driven goals, you are probably working on the wrong things. In fact, everyone in your department could be working diligently to accomplish things that have little relationship or meaning to the customer. There must be customer-oriented goals at every level of the organization, whether it is a large corporation, small business, nonprofit agency, or government institution.

To be quality-oriented in customer service, you must have:

1. A *mission* that reflects a customer orientation.
2. *Goals* that are aligned with the mission.
3. *Strategies* to achieve the goals.
4. An *attitude* of continuous quality improvement.
5. *Commitment* and *action* to make it happen.

Developing a Mission to Provide Strategic Direction

A Mission

Reflects your company's values and is usually a broad, general statement that is not measurable. It reflects the values that the organization lives by each day.

Example of a mission statement: "To produce the best quality product in our industry and to deliver it to our customers in a timely, efficient manner and to treat all of our customers—those who buy our products and our employees who produce them—with dignity and respect."

Goals

The specific strategies your company plans to develop and implement to continuously achieve your mission. Goals should be directly related to the mission. This is referred to as *alignment.*

Here are the characteristics of a meaningful goal:

Get commitment. Involve your department employees or team in setting your customer service goals. When employees are committed, they are more likely to take ownership; that is, they are more likely to consider the organization as their own and reflect that pride in their performance.

Obtainable. Be sure the goals are realistic—that they are within your capacity and resources to accomplish.

Action-oriented. The goal statement should include an action verb. Even more important than the wording is the action you take to make the goal a reality.

Leadership-driven. Remember that management sets the tone. The leaders of the organization determine how seriously employees perceive customer service goals.

Specific and measurable. It is essential to quantify goals. You must determine where you are and where you want to go.

▶**Example:**
"We will strive to decrease the customer complaints in our department from 6 complaints per 100 calls to 2 complaints per 100 calls by January 1.

Setting Customer Service Goals

Consider some goals that would make your department more effective in providing excellent customer service:

1. _____

   _____

2. _____

   _____

3. _____

   _____

4. _____

   _____

5. _____

   _____

6. _____

   _____

7. _____

   _____

8. _____

   _____

Strategies for Achieving Customer-Service Goals

Strategic planning is having a set of objectives or activities to achieve the goals that are related to your mission. In its simplest form, strategic planning simply means having a specific strategy to accomplish each of your goals.

In some companies, customer service goals exist, but there isn't a strategy or plan for achieving them. Thus, there may be a lot of discussion, fancy slogans, and fanfare about customer service, but the job of customer service never gets done. Refer back to Figure 6, which depicts the Back Slapper Customer Service Climate. In this environment, there is seemingly a great deal of attention to providing caring service, but there is little attention to follow-through. This scenario is what can happen when a goal has been set, but no strategy for accomplishing it has been determined.

Here is an example of a *strategy* for achieving a goal. Notice that it consists of a set of objectives or activities that leads to the accomplishment of the goal.

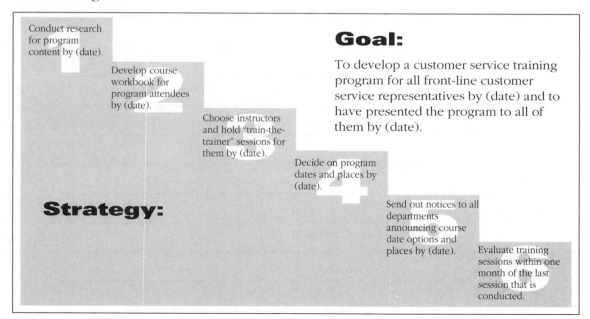

Conduct research for program content by (date).

Develop course workbook for program attendees by (date).

Choose instructors and hold "train-the-trainer" sessions for them by (date).

Decide on program dates and places by (date).

Send out notices to all departments announcing course date options and places by (date).

Evaluate training sessions within one month of the last session that is conducted.

Goal:

To develop a customer service training program for all front-line customer service representatives by (date) and to have presented the program to all of them by (date).

Strategy:

Developing Strategies to Achieve Your Goals

Select one of the goals you listed on page 42 and then write a strategy to accomplish it.

Goal: _____

_____

Strategy:

1. _____

_____

2. _____

_____

3. _____

_____

4. _____

_____

5. _____

_____

6. _____

_____

7. _____

_____

8. _____

_____

After you list your goal and strategies, be sure to share your proposal with others in your department or company who have the authority to implement it. Get their feedback so that they will feel ownership of the plan.

An Attitude of Continuous Quality Improvement

To achieve excellent customer service, you and everyone in your company must strive for quality in everything you do. This means continuously improving your procedures, attitudes, knowledge, products, services, delivery systems, and training.

Two important concepts in many organizations today are *Total Quality Management* (TQM) and *Continuous Quality Improvement (CQI)*. Some companies are using this acronym instead of TQM to reflect that improving quality is never finished—it is a continuous process. These are meaningful concepts *if* there is a devotion or commitment to follow-through.

History of Total Quality Management

The late Dr. W. Edwards Deming is credited with developing the concept of TQM. In 1950, the Japanese government asked Dr. Deming to come to Japan to help rebuild the country's industries. In the 1950s, "made in Japan" was synonymous with junk or poor quality. But in less than a generation, public perception of Japanese products changed. Consumers began to associate them with quality.

The Japanese government attributes its success, in large part, to W. Edwards Deming and his concepts. Their esteem for Dr. Deming is so

Where on the following quality continuum do you perceive your company's procedures, products, and services to be?

◀──────────────────────▶
INFERIOR   **SUPERIOR**

great that the highest quality achievement award in Japan is called the Deming Award.

What exactly did Dr. Deming teach the Japanese? Deming was a statistician who taught the Japanese the concept of *total quality control*. The Japanese changed the name of the concept to Total Quality Management. Essentially, Deming said that if you want to improve quality, you must continuously measure your progress. Therefore, it is important to set goals and to have a strategy for achieving them. In the process of carrying out your customer service goals, you must periodically check your variance from your desired results and then make corrections. In other words, correct your mistakes.

Deming also taught the Japanese that in order to improve quality, they needed to encourage and listen to their most important resources—their people! Make everyone responsible and accountable for quality. Work as a team!

Deming's concepts have shown such high results that many American companies have now embraced his ideas to strive for quality.

Commitment and Action to Making It Happen

As discussed in Chapter 4, commitment and action to making it happen are an important part of being quality-oriented. Fancy slogans and lots of buttons, balloons, and fanfare can be helpful to convey the enthusiasm surrounding your plan and follow-through. But, if that is all you have—a bunch of slogans, buttons, and balloons—your customers will see the superficiality. Remember, they want excellent *customer* service—attention to follow-through—not *lip* service.

The Deming/Shewhart cycle of Plan, Do, Check, Act (shown in Fig. 8) illustrates the idea that the goal of quality improvement must be continuous—it is a never-ending cycle.

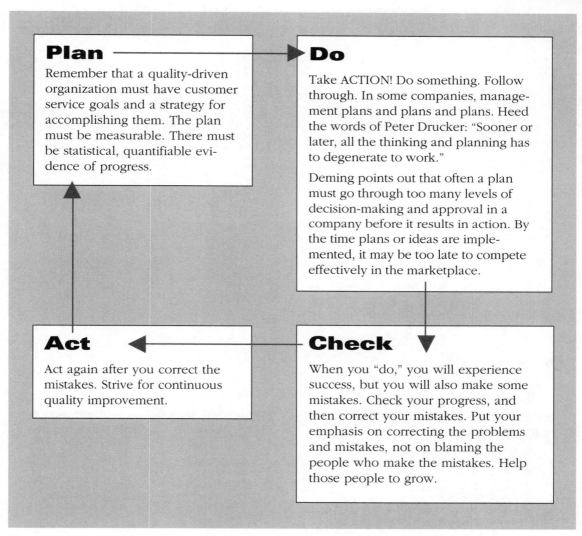

Figure 8. Deming taught that achieving quality improvement is a continuous, never-ending goal. This is illustrated in the Plan, Do, Check, Act cycle. Deming developed this concept based on what he was taught by Dr. Walter Shewhart early in his career at Bell Labs.

> ▶ *"There are three kinds of people in this world. There is a small group of people who make things happen. There is a somewhat larger group of people who watch things happen. And there is an overwhelming majority who don't have the slightest idea what is happening. The successful person is the person who makes things happen."*
>
> Nicholas Murray Butler

CHAPTER

6

The **Customer** *Service Team*

"*The difference between mediocrity and greatness is
the feeling these guys have for each other. Most
people call it team spirit. When the players are
imbued with that special feeling, you know you've
got yourself a winning team.*"

Vince Lombardi, as quoted by Lee Iaccocca
in the book *Iaccocca*

What Makes a Team a Team

Calling a team a team does not make it a team. You have to live the principles of teamwork every day. Teamwork is essential for follow-through in customer service. If you and your team work together, you can accomplish your customer service goals.

Here is the definition of a *customer service team:* Two or more people who are organized to accomplish specific goals that meet customer needs and who are committed to those goals and to fellow team members.

Broken down, the definition of a customer service team is based on three principles:

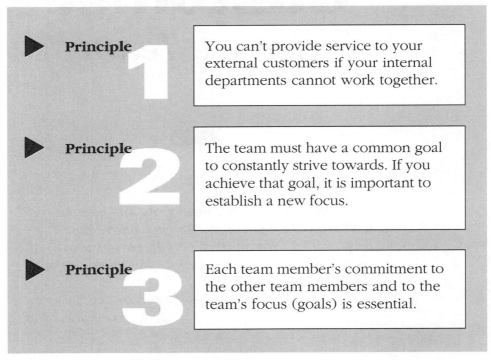

▶ **Principle** 1
You can't provide service to your external customers if your internal departments cannot work together.

▶ **Principle** 2
The team must have a common goal to constantly strive towards. If you achieve that goal, it is important to establish a new focus.

▶ **Principle** 3
Each team member's commitment to the other team members and to the team's focus (goals) is essential.

What Makes a Customer Service Team Successful?

List some characteristics that you think make a customer service team successful.

_____

_____

_____

_____

_____

_____

_____

Now, compare your answers to these six key characteristics of successful teams identified by the American Society for Training and Development:

1. **_Leadership._** Someone has to help the team define its focus.

2. **_Training._** Every team member needs to know his or her job (see Chapter 3).

3. **_Planning._** The team needs to define how it will accomplish its customer service goals (see Chapter 4).

4. **_Selection._** It is important to have the right people on your team—the best people for each job to effectively serve your customers.

5. **_Communication._** Team members need to commit to communicating clearly and concisely.

6. **_Commitment._** Team members must genuinely support each other and have a real commitment to serving internal and external customers.

Source: Patricia Galagan, _Training and Development Journal_

Your Role as a Team Player

Teamwork demands that all departments provide service to the internal customer who is on the front line serving the external customer. That means you are responsible for serving other team members and they are responsible for serving you. As a team member, you must remember that the key word to describe your relationship with others is *interdependence*. Others are dependent on you, and you are dependent on them. You need each other to ultimately serve your external customers and to meet their specific needs.

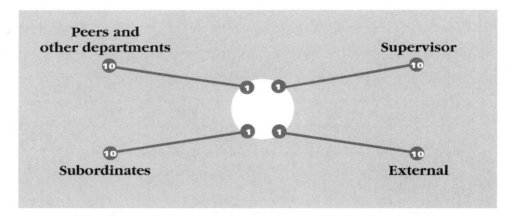

In the diagram above, place an "X" along each of the four continuums according to how well you feel you provide service to each of the customers you serve (10 is best). Remember that you are at the center of the customer service universe. Others are depending on you.

The late Sam Walton built the Wal-Mart chain into a hugely successful organization. He believed in truly serving all of his customers, both internal and external. He exemplified team atmosphere. Here are his ten rules, in his own words (italics added) from *Sam Walton: Made in America, My Story:*

Sam's Rules for Building a Business

Rule 1: *Commit to your business.* I think I overcame every single one of my personal shortcomings by the sheer passion I brought to my work.

Rule 2: *Share your profits with all associates and treat them as partners.* In turn, they will treat you as a partner, and together you will all perform beyond your wildest expectations.

Rule 3: *Motivate your partners.* Money and ownership aren't enough... Set high goals, encourage competition, and then keep score.

Rule 4: *Communicate everything you possibly can to your partners.* The more they know, the more they'll understand ... Information is power, and the gain you get from empowering your associates more than offsets the risk of informing your competitors.

Rule 5: *Appreciate everything your associates do for the business ...* Nothing else can quite substitute for a few well-chosen, well-timed, sincere words of praise.

Rule 6: *Celebrate your successes.* Find some humor in your failures. Don't take yourself so seriously.

Rule 7: *Listen to everyone in your company.* And figure out ways to get them talking. The folks on the front lines—the ones who actually talk to the customer—are the only ones who really know what's going on out there.

Rule 8: *Exceed your customers' expectations.* If you do, they'll come back over and over.

Rule 9: *Control your expenses better than your competition.* This is where you can always find the competitive advantage. You can make a lot of different mistakes and still recover if you run an efficient operation.

Rule 10: *Swim upstream.* If everyone else is doing it one way, there's a good chance you can find your niche by going in exactly the opposite direction ... I guess in all my years, what I heard more often than anything was: A town of less than 50,000 cannot support a discount store for very long.

Interdependence in Serving Your Customers

There are three service levels in every company or organization. Employees at each level are dependent on employees at the other levels. Place a check mark in the box next to the description of the level at which you operate. Then consider the traits of your customers. Being able to describe your customers' traits can help you to focus on their needs.

☐ Front-line Service Level

These individuals directly serve the external customer. They have face-to-face and telephone contact with customers who are interested in your goods and services.

If you operate at this level, describe below some of the traits of your customers:

_____

_____

_____

_____

_____

☐ Internal Service Level

These people serve the external customer by serving the internal customer (other staff and employees). People at this level may provide support services to other departments.

If you operate at this level, describe below some of the traits of your customers:

_____

_____

_____

_____

_____

☐ Management Support Level

These are the individuals who set the tone (see Chapter 2). They determine whether a true customer service climate exists in the company. They have the responsibility of serving the internal service level, the front-line service level and, ultimately, the external customer.

If you operate at this level, describe below some of the traits of your customers:

_____

_____

_____

_____

_____

Here is an example that demonstrates the concept of interdependence and why it is important to work as a team to achieve customer service goals:

> A food server in a hospital delivers a tray of food to a patient (external customer). The food server is a front-line service level person. The food server says to the patient: "Good evening, Mr. Thomas. We have a nice, warm tray of food for you." The server then places the tray on the table by the bed.
>
> Mr. Thomas takes the lid from the plate and discovers that all the food is mixed together—the peas, mashed potatoes, and gravy look like an ill-prepared casserole. The mystery meat on the plate is indiscernible and cold.
>
> Mr. Thomas wonders whether he should taste the food, but decides that since he's already in the hospital, why not! As he expected he would, Mr. Thomas discovers that the meal doesn't taste good.
>
> Who takes the brunt of the patient's complaint?

You know that it is the food server, the front-line service person. But who actually prepared the food? It was a cook, an internal service level person. The cook's customer is the food server and, in this case, the cook did not meet his customer's needs. So you begin to see how these two levels are interdependent and how they impact each other.

Who sets the tone for preparing good food and customer caring? The management support level does! The manager creates a climate in which employees are expected to serve each other and, ultimately, the external customer. The management support level knows that you prosper or perish based on how well you serve customer needs.

CHAPTER

7

Getting and **Keeping Customers:** *Marketing and Selling*

Sell good merchandise at a reasonable profit, treat your customers like human beings, and they'll always come back for more."

L.L. Bean

Lifetime Customer Value

Consider your customers in terms of their value to your business over a period of many years—or their lifetime customer value (LCV)—not just in terms of one transaction. The following example illustrates this point.

Assume that someone in your household goes to the grocery store at least once a week, spending an average of $100 each week. If you shop fifty weeks out of the year, you spend $5,000 a year at that store—and you are only one customer! Consider how many customers go in and out of the store, particularly on Saturdays—and multiply by $5,000.

Consider, too, the money that you and your fellow shoppers will spend if you patronize that store for five years. You alone will have spent at least $25,000.

But what if the store doesn't meet your needs? What if you don't receive value for the time and money you spend? You will likely shop for groceries somewhere else. The grocery store chain will have lost a valued customer—and at least $25,000. And that doesn't count the ten people you would have told not to shop there. Take the $25,000 loss of those would-be customers and you are up to $250,000 in lost revenues, assuming each customer's weekly bill averages $100.

Make a special effort to keep your customers!

Besides the money you lose in potential sales when you lose a customer, consider the money you must *spend* to recruit new customers. Rebecca Morgan offers these statistics in *Calming Upset Customers:*

- It costs six times as much to acquire a new customer as it does to keep a current one.
- It costs $19.76 to keep a current customer and $118.16 to get a new one.

Achieving Lifetime Customer Value

What are some steps you can take to keep your customers? Brainstorm with other people in your department about some of the things you can do. Take the best ideas, give them thorough consideration, and implement those that will make your customers feel like they are the best!

1. _____

2. _____

3. _____

4. _____

5. _____

6. _____

7. _____

8. _____

9. _____

10. _____

Now, compare your responses with those on the following page.

What You Can Do to Keep Your Customers

1. *Follow up and follow through.* Build trust and integrity by following through on what you said you would do to meet your customers' needs. Nothing you do will have more of an impact on building a relationship of trust.

2. *Anticipate your customers' needs.* To do this, it is important for you to focus your attention on what your customers really care about. Is it quality, timeliness, low price, easy access, or something else? If you can anticipate their needs, you can successfully serve them. Also, survey your customers periodically to find out whether what you anticipate they need is what they really want and need.

3. *Take the initiative to solve problems.* Every customer you engage—whether internal or external—has a need to be met. Many times customers express their needs as problems. A co-worker (internal customer) may need assistance with using a new software program, or an external customer may need your product or service by a certain date. Solving problems is an integral part of carrying out your customer service responsibilities.

4. *Concentrate on what you are doing.* Focus your attention on the customer. Consider your own role as a customer. Have you ever been speaking to a clerk who is supposed to be meeting your needs, but you know that he or she is not listening to a word you are saying? Customers are impressed when they sense you are concentrating on what they are telling you.

5. *CARE!* Care enough to be the best that you can be. Often grocery stores, car rental companies, department stores, gas stations, airlines, hotels, restaurants, hardware stores, and numerous other businesses look the same. When price is equal, what is the difference that causes you to choose one business over the other? It's probably the feeling you get when you leave the store or hang up the phone that says, "They really care about me!"

6. *Establish customer-driven company values.* Customers can tell the diference between companies that are customer-driven and those that are cost-driven.

Trading Value for Value

Another way to keep your customers is to give them value, a concept that was first discussed in Chapter 1. When customers give something up—usually their time or money—they want equal or greater value for their exchange. Companies and organizations that continually strive to create value are more likely to keep their customers.

Create value for your company by:

- *Offering a fair price.* If you are a for-profit company, don't gouge your customer with high prices just for the sake of charging high prices.
- *Creating goodwill.* Whether your organization is for-profit, nonprofit, or in the public sector, show customers that you are people-oriented.

 A marketing executive was backing out of her driveway one morning when she noticed the little boy next door sitting in the front yard with his dog. The dog had a sign around his neck that said "Free dog."

The marketing executive asked the little boy, "Tommy, are you getting rid of your dog?" He said that he was.

The marketing executive said, "If you really want to get rid of your dog, clean him up and give him value. Put a price tag on him!"

The next morning as she was backing out of the driveway, the marketing executive saw Tommy and his dog again in the front yard. Tommy had bathed, groomed, and perfumed the dog and put a sign around the dog's neck—"Dog for sale—$5,000."

The marketing executive was amused and thought maybe she'd overstated her point. But she drove off to work and thought nothing more about it. When she arrived home that evening, Tommy was in the front yard without his dog. Curious, she yelled out her car window, "Tommy, where is your dog?"

"I sold him," Tommy replied.

She shouted: "Very good. How much did you get for him?"

Tommy proudly announced, "$5,000!"

The marketing executive, not believing what she heard, asked quizzically, "You got $5,000 for that dog?"

Tommy looked at her and said, "Not exactly, but do you see my two new cats worth $2,500 each?"

The point of the story is that Tommy perceived value in exchanging his dog for the two cats. If each party in an exchange is satisfied, then there is, indeed, a trade of value for value.

- ***Concentrating on quality.*** Your priority must be to offer quality in every item you produce and every service you provide.
- ***Being accessible.*** Make it easy for your customers to be your customers and to stay your customers.
- ***Being well-groomed.*** Your customers form an impression of you within about one minute of meeting you. You want to create a powerful first impression.
- ***Communicating effectively and confidently.*** Customers respect employees who can convey the features and benefits of a company's products and services. Imagine yourself in a restaurant. Do you prefer a waiter or waitress who tells you about the special of the day in a knowledgeable way, looking you in the eye and explaining it completely and easily? Or do you prefer someone who seems ill at ease, unsure, and forgets to tell you about part of the special?
- ***Using technical devices to streamline your business and to make it more accessible.*** Consider installing additional phone lines, fax machines, and computers. Keep in mind, however, that these devices are meant to make you and your company more accessible. Be cautious about losing face-to-face or voice-to-voice contact with your customers by hiding behind these devices.

12 Ways to Offer Customers Value

What else can you do to offer your customers value?

1. _____

   _____

2. _____

   _____

3. _____

   _____

4. _____

   _____

5. _____

   _____

The Importance of Managed Perception

Peter Drucker defines quality in a product or service as "not what the supplier puts in. It is what the customer gets out and is willing to pay for. Customers only pay for what is of use to them and gives them value. Nothing else constitutes quality."

The idea, of course, is that you must focus on producing the best quality goods and services possible. Your customers must be able to perceive that the quality of the goods and services you offer is of the same or better value as the time, money, and effort they will have to put out to obtain them.

If your customers have a positive image of your company and your goods and services, they will likely keep coming back to you because they know they can depend on you to meet their needs with quality. (Again, they perceive value in what you have to offer.)

What is image? It is a managed *perception*. Sometimes it is referred to as *positioning*—establishing yourself and your company in a certain way in the minds of your customers. In other words, influencing how your customers feel about you and your organization. Many times companies do this through advertising. Sometimes, as an individual, you can create the image or managed perception by how you treat your customers. If your customers' perception of you and your company is positive and trusting—that is, they perceive that you will offer them quality (value)— they are likely to continue to do business with you. Simply stated, customers must perceive that they are receiving a *benefit* by patronizing your organization.

Types of Benefits

▶ **Explicit benefits:**

> Those that are easily noticeable, such as highly attentive personal service provided by a restaurant.

▶ **Implicit benefits:**

> A more subtle aspect of the service, such as when the maitre-d' calls you by name and remembers your food preferences.

Explicit benefits are what you advertise to get the customers to call or frequent the business. Implicit benefits are what you provide to keep customers coming back.

13 Managed Perception

What managed perception do you want your customers to have of your company?

_____

What do you offer in terms of quality—and, therefore, value—that would keep your customers loyal to you?

1. _____
   _____

2. _____
   _____

3. _____
   _____

4. _____
   _____

5. _____
   _____

6. _____
   _____

7. _____
   _____

8. _____
   _____

9. _____
   _____

10. _____
    _____

Improving Your Selling Skills: Relationship Selling

Relationship selling is the idea of building rapport, or a trusting relationship, with your customers so that they feel good about buying goods from you or using your goods and services.

Companies that don't build positive relationships with their customers and that provide poor customer service average only a 1 percent return on sales. They also see their market share erode at an average annual rate of 2 percent according to the publication *Office Hours* (Issue No. 249). If you work in a government or nonprofit organization, you probably don't lose market share (although you certainly can in a nonprofit organization if a donor decides to contribute funds to another organization because he or she perceives the service of the current nonprofit organization to be poor). But what you do lose is goodwill among your clients and customers. When you make no attempt to build relationships or if you show indifference towards customers, they sense it and will likely go somewhere else where they feel the company cares about them.

Here's what you can do to build positive relationships with customers:

1. ***Call your customers by name.*** But don't overuse names because it sounds patronizing. Do let your customers know that you aren't just trying to sell your goods and services. Convey to them that you are trying to create a friendship—a customer for life.

2. ***Get customers to talk about themselves.*** But don't pry. Usually all you need to do is ask people a couple of questions about themselves as you make "small talk," and they'll offer information about their circumstances and ambitions.

3. ***Share your background and ambitions with your customers when you have something in common with them.*** Doing so builds a bridge between you and the customer. Don't talk about yourself too much, but do be friendly.

4. ***Let your customers know that you will be there for them after the sale or transaction.*** Communicate that they can call you or see you whenever they have a question or concern.

5. ***Always be willing to listen and to answer customers' questions, even if they aren't buying today.*** The relationship you build with your customers today will have an influence on what they buy tomorrow. Always be sure to thank your customers for their interest.

Selling Yourself and Your Company

Selling is the presentation (communication) and promotion of products and services in such a way that customers are willing and excited to trade value for value or make an exchange.

We are all salespeople in one sense or another. We are all selling ourselves, our company, and our products and services each day. Whether it is face to face, by telephone or in writing, selling is an essential part of excellent customer service. Here are some key factors related to selling:

1. ***Believe in yourself.*** Many people have programmed themselves for failure. They don't believe in themselves; they lack self-confidence. But you can't sell anything to someone else if you aren't sold on yourself. Concentrate on what you know you can do and find strength in it.

2. ***Continuously seek knowledge.*** Strive for continuous quality improvement on a personal basis (see Chapter 3). Knowledge gives you power. Power gives you authority. Authority will give you self-confidence over time.

 Tom Hopkins, a well-known sales trainer and speaker, wrote a classic book on selling called *How to Master the Art of Selling.* Here is what he said about handling rejection:

1. Never see failure as failure, but only as a learning experience.
2. Never see failure as failure, but only as the negative feedback needed to change your course or direction.
3. Never see failure as failure, but only as the opportunity to develop your sense of humor.
4. Never see failure as failure, but only as the opportunity to practice your techniques and perfect your performance.
5. Never see failure as failure, but only as the game you must play to win.

3. ***Sell yourself first.*** Customers need to know they can trust you. Create a relationship. Break down barriers. Let customers know you are "for real" and you have their interests in mind. Are you thinking about the money you will make, or the customers you will help? Consider the money you make as one of the rewards for helping customers.

4. ***Reward your customers.*** Thank them for their purchases and ideas. Reward them by asking for their opinions on the quality of your service and on how you can improve your products and services.

5. ***Be persistent.*** Don't be put off by rejection. Any job in customer service requires tenacity.

▶ President Calvin Coolidge said: "Press on. Nothing in the world can take the place of persistence. Talent will not. Nothing is more common than unsuccessful men with talent. Genius will not. Unrewarded genius is almost a proverb. Education alone will not. The world is full of educated derelicts. Persistence and determination alone are omnipotent."

Rating Your Selling Skills

There are some skills that are essential to effective selling. To find out how well you possess these skills, rate yourself on a scale of 1 to 10. A "1" indicates a need for drastic improvement. A "10" symbolizes excellence.

1. **Product knowledge:** How well do you know the features and benefits of your products or service?

   1 • • • 5 • • • • 10

2. **Listening:** How well do you listen and show to your customers that you are listening?

   1 • • • 5 • • • • 10

3. **Trust-building:** How well do you demonstrate that you are trustworthy?

   1 • • • • 5 • • • • 10

4. **Encouraging feedback:** How well do you let your customers know that you value their questions, advice, and information?

   1 • • • 5 • • • • 10

5. **Interpreting customer needs:** How well do you listen for what customers really need when they aren't telling you directly?

   1 • • • 5 • • • • 10

6. **Projecting an image of excellence:** How well do you position yourself and your company in the minds of your customers—in other words, how well do you manage the perception of your customer?

   1 • • • 5 • • • • 10

7. **Reading nonverbal signals:** How well do you read body language to determine how comfortable your customers are in opening up to you?

   1 • • • 5 • • • • 10

8. ***Knowing how and when to sell features and benefits:*** How well do you assess when you should push harder or back off in selling your goods and services?

1 • • • 5 • • • • 10

9. ***Probing and diagnosing:*** How good are you at asking meaningful questions to determine customers' needs?

1 • • • 5 • • • • 10

CHAPTER

8

Handling **Customer** *Complaints*

"If a company that is supposed to be operating in a service industry has a department called the customer service department, what are all the other departments supposed to be doing?"

Karl Albrecht and Ron Zemke
Service America

71

Be Glad They Told You!

Don't complaints seem to come in clusters? Everything will seem to run smoothly for awhile, and then one day the complaints just start streaming in. Sometimes when this happens, employees become defensive, but what they really should do is "look, listen, and learn." Be glad the customer came to *you* with the complaint. If customers don't tell you why they're unhappy, they will likely tell someone else, which not only strips you of the opportunity to fix the complaint but also drives potential customers away.

Think about it. If you've had a bad customer service experience in a restaurant, hotel, car dealership, dry cleaners, department store, or other business, wouldn't you more likely tell your friends than the employees of the company where the problem was created?

Why do we have this tendency? Because complaining often takes too long, is a hassle, or may be embarrassing. We may also think that if the company doesn't care, then why should we care about conveying our unhappiness? We'll just take our business elsewhere.

Consider the following widely quoted statistics from the White House Office on Consumer Affairs, Technical Assistance Research Program:

- *Ninety-six percent* of unhappy customers never complain to you. (They tell everyone else.)

- *Ninety-one percent* of those who don't complain won't buy again from the business that offended them. (In a government or nonprofit business, a customer may have no choice, but the customer is likely to be unfriendly and uncooperative.)

- The average unhappy customer will share the negative experience with at least *nine* other people. Rebecca Morgan's book *Calming Upset Customers* points out that an unhappy customer will tell at least eleven other people. Each of those people will in turn tell five more people, so that sixty-seven people are eventually aware of the original complaint (1 + 11 + 55 = 67).

- *Thirteen percent* will tell more than twenty people.
- The average happy customer will remember the incident for *eighteen* months.
- The average unhappy customer will remember the incident for *23-1/2 years*.

BE GLAD THAT UNHAPPY CUSTOMERS TELL YOU so that you can do something about it.

Why Do Customers Complain?

Some people are chronic complainers. However, most people speak up only if they have a truly legitimate concern. And then, keep in mind, that they will complain only if it is easy for them to do so. Usually when a customer is concerned enough to complain, he or she has a good reason. And when a number of customers complain about the same thing, that tends to validate the complaint. At that point, you had better take corrective action.

At Xerox Corporation, executives spend one day a month taking complaints from customers about machines, bills, and services. This way they stay close to customers.

Why Do Your Customers Complain?

Here are several common reasons why customers complain. Check the ones that may apply to you, based on feedback you have received from your customers.

1. They have had to wait a long time.
2. They feel they were treated rudely.
3. The product or service lacks quality.
4. They feel overwhelmed or confused.
5. They have a difficult time getting through on the telephone.
6. They have a difficult time understanding the language.
7. They have been treated poorly by someone else in your company.
8. They are frustrated or tired.
9. They feel they are being patronized.
10. They feel they are talked down to.
11. They feel that no one is listening to them.
12. They are in a hurry.

What are some other reasons for complaining that your customers have given you?

_____

_____

_____

_____

Now, choose something on the list that you have checked and take action to correct it.

What to Do When Customers Complain

Don't allow yourself or anyone else in the company to get caught up in the "Hey, it's not my job" mentality. When it comes to serving customers, it's everybody's job to make it right and do it right.

Here are seven steps for responding effectively to customer complaints:

1. ***Don't interrupt.*** Let the customer finish when there is a complaint. Few things will exacerbate the problem more than interrupting an emotional customer.

2. ***Listen attentively.*** Listen for meaning. When customers are upset, angry, or concerned, they might not specifically express their real needs. Remember that customer service is about meeting needs. Customers may talk all around what they really need, so you must listen "between the lines" sometimes. This is called *sorting* because you are sorting out a customer's emotional statements from what he or she really means and wants.

3. ***Use feedback.*** Repeat the complaint back to the customer to be sure you have correctly identified it. You can't solve the problem if you don't know the real problem.

4. ***Apologize.*** Apologies should be brief, sincere, and future-oriented. They should be brief for two reasons: (1) the longer the apology, the more patronizing it begins to sound and (2) when you are dealing with aggressive customers, they may become more aggressive when they realize that you are vulnerable. To be future-oriented means to move toward solving the problem ("I'm sorry that happened. Let's see how we can solve this problem.").

5. ***Discuss alternatives for solving the problem.*** Explain the kind of action you will take to handle the complaint effectively and in a timely fashion.

6. ***Get customer confirmation.*** Be sure that the customer *understands* the action you will take so that he or she can anticipate the proposed outcome.

7. ***Say thank you.*** Even when customers complain or are angry, it is important to thank them for reporting the complaint. Remember, they cared enough and took the time to let you know their concerns.

▶ *"You gotta get out there.
You have to talk to the
people. You have to listen
to them mostly. You have
to make them know that
this is a partnership."*

Sam Walton

Coping With
Difficult
Customers

"Contempt, we feel, is the biggest barrier to sustainable, superior, performance in hospitals, schools, banks, retailing and manufacturing companies. We stress contempt because it's the outgrowth of attitude ... common decency, common courtesy toward the customer is the exception."

Tom Peters and Nancy Austin
A Passion for Excellence

Coping With Angry Customers

When a customer is angry, how should you handle the situation? Place a check mark next to the answer you think is correct.

☐ Agree with the customer

☐ Become angry

☐ Walk away or hang up the phone

☐ Point out to the customer that he or she is being rude

☐ Remain calm and focus on the problem

The correct answer is to remain calm. Stay calm and concentrate on solving the problem.

In a situation in which the customer is "on the attack," your natural tendency is to protect yourself or to avoid dealing with the problem. Stress management experts refer to this as the "fight or flight" syndrome. You either fight back and defend yourself, or you flee the situation.

What is not natural is to remain calm. Remaining calm is learned behavior. It must be practiced. The more you practice, the better you get; you then tend to minimize fighting with or fleeing from your customers. If you can remain calm, you can more readily meet the needs of the customer as well as your own needs.

Here are some tips for remaining calm in difficult customer service situations:

- ***Control your breathing.*** In stressful situations, breathing becomes rapid and you can feel out of control. Take two or three deep breaths.

- ***Listen for the customer's real message.*** A customer who is upset is emotional and may use words and phrases that aren't really meant. If you take the verbal attack personally, you will be more inclined to defend yourself and fight back. Sort out the customer's emotional message from his or her real message and need.

Example:

A customer has tried to call you several times, but has been unable to reach you because you've been in a meeting. When he finally reaches you, he says, emotionally, "I've tried to call you a hundred times." That is an emotional statement. What is the customer's real message and need? "I'm frustrated because I haven't been able to talk with you, and I have a problem that needs to be solved."

Don't respond to the customer's emotional statement by defending yourself and saying "Come on, sir, a hundred times!" If you do, you will be responding to the wrong message. A way to respond to the customer's real need is to remain calm and simply say: "I was in a meeting, but I would be pleased to assist you now. Please tell me about your concern."

- ***Stay focused on what you can do for the customer, not on what you can't do.*** Try to use words like, "I can," "I will," "will you" instead of "I can't do that," " I won't," "It's against company policy," "You will have to" or other phrases that will only further anger the customer.

Example:

Customer:	"I want the delivery by Friday at noon."
Your response:	"I know I can have it to you by Monday at 10:00 a.m."
Don't say:	"There's no way we can get it to you by Friday."

- ***Be aware of your body language in face-to-face situations.*** Don't inadvertently send negative messages that will further anger a customer. Avoid negative facial expressions, closed stances (arms folded), or confrontational stances (toe-to-toe).

- ***Be aware of voice tone in face-to-face situations or in telephone conversations.*** If you raise your voice or sound sarcastic or agitated, it may rile your customer even more.

How well do you control your emotions in difficult customer situations? Some customers can really "get the best of you" if you let them. Granted, it's not easy to maintain a relaxed mood when you are dealing with difficult customers. Your tendency may be to become emotional. But you will be much better served and be able to serve others more effectively if you control your emotions.

If you can keep your emotions under control, you can help customers bring their anger under control so you can work together toward a solution. Here's how to calm an upset customer:

- ***Don't interrupt or disagree with the angry person.*** That will only exacerbate the problem. Let the customer vent, as long as he or she doesn't ramble on and on or become hostile. Hint: If you are dealing with someone who is going on and on, seize any moment when the person pauses. Then say: "Excuse me. Let me see if I understand correctly. Point number one is…; point number two is…; I would appreciate if I could have point number three clarified for me."

  This is called leading. You are bringing the customer back to the problem and leading him or her to the next point.

- ***Paraphrase what the customer tells you.*** Let the customer know you are listening. Test yourself to be sure you received the message the customer sent.

  ### Example:
  "Let me make sure I understand correctly. You were promised a phone call on Friday on the status of your delivery, and you didn't receive the phone call. Is that correct?"

- ***Acknowledge the complaint.*** Show understanding. See the customer's point of view.

- ***Encourage the angry person to help you solve the problem.*** Be sure to focus on the problem as soon as you can. But don't rush the customer.

- ***Arrive at a specific solution.*** Be sure to clearly and specifically communicate it to your customer.

- Here is a hint to supervisors: ***Empower front-line employees and working supervisors to make decisions and solve problems at the front line.*** It angers customers more if the employee has to put them on hold or keep them waiting while the employee gets approval from the "higher-ups."

How Well Do You Handle Difficult Customers?

The self-assessment that follows will give you an idea of how well you handle difficult customer situations. Circle the number that you feel best describes your behavior regarding each statement. A "1" means "usually." A "5" means "never."

	Usually				Never
1. I express to that customer what I can do rather than what I can't do.	1	2	3	4	5
2. I am good at following through on what I say I will do.	1	2	3	4	5
3. I see the customer's point of view.	1	2	3	4	5
4. I smile, when appropriate, and have a relaxed and open body position.	1	2	3	4	5
5. I am in control when a customer is cursing or using demeaning language.	1	2	3	4	5
6. I am quick to apologize if my company or I have done something wrong or if we have not followed through.	1	2	3	4	5
7. I thank customers when they bring a problem or concern to my attention.	1	2	3	4	5
8. I am comfortable with silent pauses in conversations with customers.	1	2	3	4	5
9. I become very nervous when customers are upset with me or my company.	1	2	3	4	5
10. I focus on listening intently when the customer is upset.	1	2	3	4	5

Confrontations: Positive versus Negative

We have a tendency to think of confrontations as negative experiences. And they can be if you confront a person with the goal of causing that person to "lose." Instead, treat confrontations as positive experiences—confront problems, not people. Deal positively with the person who is involved with the problem.

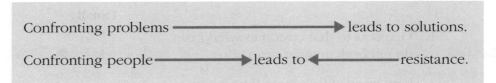

Here are several ways to confront difficult problems or situations:

- **Use diplomacy.** Find something you can agree on. If you can legitimately agree with the other person on at least one point, he or she is less likely to be confrontational. Thus, you are more likely to solve the problem.

  Example:
  "I agree with you. The order should have been filled by last Friday, based on the facts we have before us."

- **Be gentle.** Try the "feel, felt, found" approach. Find a point on which you can take action with the customer and then work at persuading him or her of the solution or change.

  Example:
  I can understand how you feel about the increase in the price. I've felt the same way before myself. I've found, though, that the quality will far outweigh the difference in price."

- **Be firm.** In this situation, you are more forceful. It is important to challenge the facts (not the person) and to correct them, if necessary.

  Example:
  "I am sure the shipment is due in on Friday at noon. I will be pleased to call you when it arrives."

- **Be direct.** State the facts directly. Be firm in your stance, and state the facts clearly. Keep your statements positive and focused on how you can be helpful.

  ### Example:

  "I know we can put you on the next flight, which leaves at 3:30 p.m." (The passenger has demanded to be on the present flight, which is overbooked).

  Don't say: "There's no way we can get you this flight. It is overbooked." (This approach is negative and cold.)

Collaboration: The Way to Solve Problems

Remember that confronting problems is the first step in solving them. Then, as solutions for solving the problem are proposed, *collaboration,* or *compromise,* should be the goal. Collaboration is a discussion between you and the customer with the goal of solving the problem to the satisfaction of both the customer and you (or your company).

A key point to keep in mind is that although collaboration is a goal that you should always strive for, it is not likely that you will always solve a customer complaint to the satisfaction of both you and the customer. Figure 9 illustrates the concept of collaboration as well as several other problem-solving alternatives.

For example, Quadrant I illustrates a win-lose approach to problem-solving, competition. In this approach, there is a high concern for yourself and your company needs, but little concern for the customer's needs. You begin to compete with the customer to prove you are right and insist that the customer must comply with your demands (see the "Hand Slapper" diagram on page 34). Of course, you lose the customer when you use this approach.

 In a survey by the Forum Corporation of 2,374 customers from fourteen organizations, more than 40 percent listed poor service as the number one reason for switching to a competitor. Only 8 percent listed price. Conclusion: People are more concerned about how they are treated than about getting the absolute best price.

Avoidance is demonstrated in Quadrant II. When you avoid the problem, you show low concern for the customer or yourself to solve the problem. Some people prefer to avoid problems because they feel uncomfortable in confronting. The problem continues unsolved.

Accommodation, illustrated in Quadrant III, is characterized by low concern for yourself and high concern for the customer in solving the problem. You may compromise yourself and your company when you don't need to. Using this approach can also make you appear patronizing to the customer.

Finally, Quadrant IV shows the ideal problem-solving approach, collaboration. A person who is willing to collaborate shows high concern for both the company and the customer in solving the problem. The goal is to solve the problem to the satisfaction of both parties. Achieving this is often referred to as creating a "win-win" solution. This approach relies on *assertive* behavior rather than on *aggressive* behavior.

Collaborative behavior requires:

- Patience.
- Effective listening.
- Negotiation.
- Calmness.
- Resolve.
- Tenacity.
- Friendliness.
- A desire to solve the problem.
- Fairness.
- Cooperation.

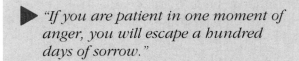

> *"If you are patient in one moment of anger, you will escape a hundred days of sorrow."*
>
> Chinese proverb

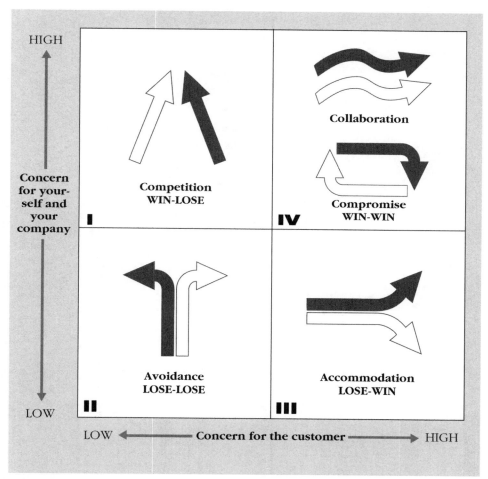

Figure 9. This conflict resolution model illustrates several approaches to problem solving. Quadrant IV is what you should strive for in solving customer problems.

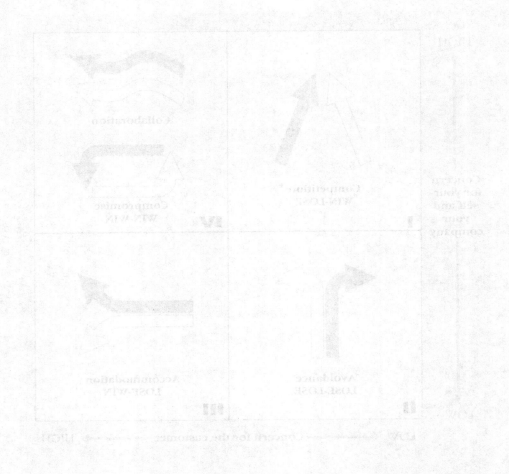

CHAPTER 10

Communicating **Effectively** With Customers

"The communicator is the person who can make himself clear to himself first."

Paul D. Griffith

How Well Do You Communicate With Your Customers?

One of the keys to providing excellent customer service is effective communication. With regard to customer service, *communication* is this: If you are the speaker, the customer receives the same message you intended; if the customer is speaking, you receive the same message the customer intended.

How well do you communicate with your customers? The following assessment will help you to determine how well you are communicating.

Communications Assessment

	Need Improvement				Excellent
1. I am careful not to jump to conclusions when the customer is speaking.	1	2	3	4	5
2. I listen for intent rather than just to the words the customer says.	1	2	3	4	5
3. I am well prepared before communicating with others.	1	2	3	4	5
4. I paraphrase what I think I've heard the customer say.	1	2	3	4	5
5. I pay attention to the customer's tone of voice and body language.	1	2	3	4	5
6. I keep my customers well informed about changes.	1	2	3	4	5
7. I ask customers to paraphrase what they have heard.	1	2	3	4	5

8. I don't resist new ideas for change before hearing the customer's proposal and position.   1   2   3   4   5

9. I don't make prejudgments about the customer.   1   2   3   4   5

10. I am willing to admit mistakes.   1   2   3   4   5

11. I am careful not to exaggerate issues— positively or negatively.   1   2   3   4   5

12. I usually use positive words in communicating.   1   2   3   4   5

13. I am careful not to be aggressive, overwhelming others.   1   2   3   4   5

14. I am cautious about not planning a response in my mind before the customer is finished talking.   1   2   3   4   5

15. I am not distracted by the customer's appearance.   1   2   3   4   5

16. I keep written communications to my customers brief and to the point.   1   2   3   4   5

17. I don't speak too fast or too slowly.   1   2   3   4   5

18. I frequently use open-ended questions to stimulate conversation with my customers.   1   2   3   4   5

19. I mentally commit to listening to the other person.   1   2   3   4   5

20. I am aware of my voice tone and how it affects customers.   1   2   3   4   5

Scoring: Total your points. Each number you circled is worth its face value. For example, a "4" is worth 4 points.

80—100	You have excellent communication skills with your customers.
60—79	Very good
40—59	Fair
under 40	You need practice.

How well did you do on the communications assessment? If you analyze your responses, you might discover that you are good at presenting your ideas, but maybe not as effective at listening to your customers. Or, vice versa. Perhaps your body language is most effective, but your voice tone may need improvement.

Set a goal to become a well-rounded communicator.

Methods of Communication

There are several ways that we really communicate:

▶ **Words**

Do you use user-friendly words—those the customer will really understand? Different people attach different meanings to words.

Example: If you tell someone to turn *down* the air-conditioning, will that person adjust the thermostat to make the room warmer or cooler? It depends on the person's perspective.

▶ **Tone of Voice**

Your voice tone will tell a customer a great deal about how you feel about yourself and your company. Your tone may even reflect how you feel about him or her. On the telephone, voice tone is critical because it is the most important means for you to make an impression.

▶ **Body Language**

Research in communications has shown that you communicate what you really mean through body language. Your words and tone of voice may say one thing, but your real message comes through in your body language—your stance, your facial expressions, and your other physical movements.

▶ **Listening**

Most of customer service communication requires listening to the customer and focusing on customer needs. About 45 percent of communication involves listening. Obviously, then, if you want to communicate effectively with your customers, you must develop this communication skill.

▶ **Attitude**

As the old saying goes, "Your attitude will determine your altitude"— how far up the corporate ladder you will go. The late Earl Nightingale, a well-known author and speaker, said that attitude is a reflection of self-esteem. If you feel good about yourself, you are more likely to feel good about your job and your customers.

Using Words Effectively

Remember to use user-friendly language when speaking to your customers. Here are some suggestions:

- *Use user-friendly words.* These are words the customer understands. Instead of trying to impress customers with big words and technical terminology, concentrate on communicating. Remember, communication means that the other person receives the message you intend; therefore, if you use words the customer doesn't understand, you won't communicate.

- *Keep acronyms —words formed from the first letter of each word in a phrase (NASA, National Aeronautics and Space Administration)—to a minimum.* Acronyms are sometimes used to shorten communication. While they can be helpful to people inside your company who know what they mean, your customers may not understand what the letters stand for. Remember that sometimes this is true of company employees as well, especially if the acronyms are specific to your department.

- *Avoid "filler" words.* These are words people use to fill a gap of silence. Because people are often uncomfortable with silence, they tend to fill it by saying something, and often what they say is inappropriate. If you feel uncomfortable with silence when you are talking with a customer, ask a question that encourages the customer to talk: "How do you feel about this solution?"

- *Use "I" instead of "you" when you communicate.* "I need your help" or "Let me see if I understand" softens your communication, but still allows you to be direct in making your point. Avoid terms such as *"You* will have to complete this report," *"You* don't understand" (one of the most condescending phrases in the English language), and *"You* will have to comply."

- *Avoid negative "trigger" words.* These are words that trigger a negative response in others or that make others defensive. Avoid saying "You're wrong," "I disagree with you," or "Where did you come up with that idea?" Of course, you should also avoid name-calling and using other labels.

- *Avoid "false positives."* These are also called "ulterior transactions." A false positive is a phrase people use to say one thing when they really mean something else. For example, a person who says, "I'll take care of this" may really be saying: "Leave me alone. Go away. I don't want to deal with this right now."

▶ **WASTED WORDS =**
Lip Service, Not _Customer_ Service

A flight attendant speaking on the public address system told the passengers that she and the other attendants would be passing out free headsets so passengers could listen to the music of their choice.

A few minutes later, the pilot announced that he would be pointing out sites of interest along the flight route. The passengers took both the flight attendant and the pilot at their "word."

One passenger's headset didn't work. The passenger pressed the flight attendant call button for assistance. No one came. He pressed it again … and again … and again. About 20 minutes later, a flight attendant showed up. The passenger explained the problem. She responded that the sound system on that passenger's side of the airplane wasn't operating. Then she walked away.

Late in the flight, the pilot finally did announce a point of interest. The only problem was that cloud cover prevented the passengers from seeing the site, and the pilot's words were garbled by the ineffective sound system.

At the conclusion of the flight, the head flight attendant announced that she hoped the passengers enjoyed the music, never acknowledging that half the people had no opportunity to enjoy the entertainment.

Wasted words? Although the attendant and the pilot certainly followed their plan, they didn't follow through with quality. They would have served the passengers better had they saved their "words" and quietly delivered effective, quality service. The passengers were not impressed with their words alone.

Monitoring Your Tone of Voice

Scenario #1: You went to a sporting event last night and you didn't get home until after midnight. You are tired this morning. What should you do to reflect enthusiasm and caring to your customers?

Scenario #2: It's been one of those days! You've handled a number of complaint calls, and you're beginning to think if you have to deal with one more, you're going to scream. What should you do?

Scenario #3: The customer standing in front of you can't make up his mind. First he wants one product. Then he changes his mind. He's now considering what to do for the fourth time. Your patience is wearing thin. What should you do?

The answer, in each situation, is this: BE AWARE. That is, be aware of your behavior, your actions, and your voice tone when you are speaking. Constantly monitor yourself so that you *know* when your frustration, anger, impatience, or intolerance is becoming too great. If you don't monitor yourself, you will not have a sense of how emotional you may have become, but your customers will hear it in your voice. If you can learn to be aware of your feelings and keep them under control as you deal with customers, then perhaps later you can release hostility, anxiety, or anger to a co-worker. This is an effective and more appropriate way of venting your feelings.

Here are some factors to consider as you strive to monitor your voice tone:

- ***Be sure your voice tone is nondefensive.*** Sometimes when people are on the defensive, their voices change but they don't realize it.

- ***Be energetic.*** Even if you were out late the night before and didn't get enough sleep, concentrate on projecting an upbeat, energetic voice tone. When people are tired or disgusted, their voice tone sounds whiny.

- ***Be expressive.*** Using voice inflections helps to avoid a monotone voice. But remember to avoid sounding phony or contrived.

- **Be aware of how rapidly you speak.** Don't talk too fast or to slow. Annunciate your words so that the other person can understand what you're saying.
- **Strive for resonance.** Try lowering the pitch of your voice a little, particularly if you have a high-pitched voice. Lowering your voice, especially on the phone, will give your voice more richness and a sound of authority.
- **Be aware of your volume.** Many people speak very loudly but don't know it. Timid people have a tendency to speak too softly. Control your volume along with your resonance.
- **Smile.** Believe it or not, a smile stretches your vocal cords, which gives you greater voice resonance.
- **Temper your enthusiasm.** Too much enthusiasm can sound contrived and be interpreted as phony or patronizing. Promote, certainly, but temper your enthusiasm.

Communicating Through Body Language

The primary way we communicate to our customers in face-to-face situations is through body language. This is supported by the findings of researchers at UCLA who have discovered that we communicate in the following ways:

- Words   7%
- Tone of voice   38%
- Body language   55%

In other words, even if we use the right words and the proper tone of voice, our body language makes the biggest impression when we deliver our messages. For example, imagine that you are conducting a meeting. Throughout the meeting, one person sits with her arms folded, looking out the window, contributing nothing to the meeting. At the conclusion of the meeting, she says to you: "I really enjoyed the meeting. Thanks for inviting me." Although this woman used the right words and tone of voice, did you believe her spoken message? Probably not. Why? Because her body language during the meeting conveyed a stronger message: "I am bored" or "I am preoccupied."

Here are some tips to remember about body language, particularly in face-to-face customer situations:

- **Be aware of your facial expressions.** Some people are unaware that they frown or distort their faces when they speak. Sometimes they do this because they are nervous.

- **Make eye contact with your customers.** Don't overpower your customers or make them feel uncomfortable, but do let them know you are concentrating on them. Follow the lead of your customers. If they make considerable eye contact, you do the same. If they don't, then give them a "mental break"; that is, look away periodically when a customer is talking to you so that you don't appear to be staring the person down. Sometimes when customers are trying to explain their situation, they can be intimidated by an employee who continues to look at them. It is important to break eye contact periodically during the conversation.

- **Put yourself at the same physical level as the customer.** If your customer is standing, you should stand too. Or, ask the customer to be seated with you. The idea is to put your customer at the same level you're on. If you are dealing with an angry or difficult customer and you are seated behind a desk, move from behind the desk and toward the customer. Don't allow the desk to serve as a physical barrier.

- **Sit or stand with an open posture.** Allow your arms to rest comfortably at your sides. An open posture lets your customers know that you are receptive to their ideas, that you genuinely care and want to assist.

- **Lean forward a little.** Leaning inward suggests your interest and shows your desire to listen.

- **Be aware of physical closeness.** While learning inward can be helpful, be careful not to overdo it. Americans like space. Sitting too close to your customer may create irritation. Of course, never touch a customer, even if it's just a pat on the back, unless he or she gives you a signal that it is okay to.

- **Nod your head.** Nodding your head shows that you agree or are on the same wavelength as your customer. On the telephone, you can "nod your head" by periodically saying "yes" or "uh-huh."

The Power of Effective Listening

Here are some tips that can help you to become a better listener. They are based on studies performed at the former Sperry Corporation:

- *Spend more than 50 percent of your time listening.* Also, don't offer your opinion until you've given the other person a chance to air his or her views first.
- *Listen for ideas, not just for facts.* Listening only for facts often prevents you from grasping the speaker's meaning.
- *Avoid jumping to conclusions.* In other words, don't anticipate what the speaker is trying to say.
- *Concentrate on staying interested in what the other person is saying, even if the delivery is boring, wordy, or emotional.* Try not to let your mind wander. Listening can be difficult—you have to work at it.
- *Don't evaluate or judge how something is said.* Keep listening for ideas. Avoid becoming upset by strong words the customer may use to irritate you.
- *Never rush or interrupt the other person.* Don't change the subject until you're sure the other person has finished.
- *Ask questions to clarify points and to let the other person know you're paying attention.* Doing so will ensure that you've received the message the speaker intended.
- *Tell yourself that everyone is important enough to listen to.* Don't discount what people have to say because of their position, appearance, or social status. Really listen to every person.
- *Stay focused.* This means *concentrate*. Concentration is the key to listening. There is a big difference between listening and hearing. The difference is assimilation; that is, when you listen, you are processing what you are hearing. At this moment, because you are concentrating on reading this book, you may hear things around you but may not be assimilating them. Now sit back for a moment and listen to the sounds around you. Concentrate on them. Perhaps you hear the clicking of a computer keyboard, maybe a printer, people talking, the air conditioner, or the heater blower. Until you concen-

trated on those things, you probably heard them but weren't paying attention to them. When you listen to a customer, it is important to stay focused through concentration and assimilation.

- **_Take notes._** You are more likely to concentrate if you write information down. Of course, just list main points and key information. If you are speaking on the telephone, always be sure to let the customer know you are taking notes. Telling the customer you are taking notes lets him or her know you are interested. Also, if the customer is speaking too fast, you can remind him or her to slow down. Otherwise, you won't be able to really listen!

18

How Well Do You Listen To Your Customers?

	Most of the time	Sometimes	Seldom
1. I physically face customers (in non-telephone situations) to make sure I can hear them.	☐	☐	☐
2. I focus all my attention on the customer.	☐	☐	☐
3. I make judgments about the customer's appearance and gestures to determine whether the customer's message is worthwhile.	☐	☐	☐
4. I listen, particularly for ideas and underlying feelings.	☐	☐	☐
5. I try to eliminate my own biases.	☐	☐	☐
6. I keep my mind on what the customer is saying.	☐	☐	☐
7. I interrupt immediately if I feel the customer's statement is wrong.	☐	☐	☐
8. I take into consideration the customer's point of view before responding.	☐	☐	☐
9. I try to have the last word.	☐	☐	☐
10. I consciously evaluate the logic and credibility of what the customer says.	☐	☐	☐

For statements 1, 2, 4, 5, 6, 8, and 10, give yourself 10 points if you checked "most of the time," 5 points for "sometimes," and 0 points for "seldom."

Total _____

For statements 3, 7, and 9, give yourself 0 points for "most of the time," 5 points for "sometimes," and 10 points for "seldom."

Total _____

Scoring: Below 70: You have developed some bad listening habits.

70 to 85: You listen well, but could improve.

86+: You are an excellent listener.

Attitude: Another Important Way You Communicate

You are the message when you communicate with someone; it's not just the words you choose to send to the other person that make up the message. You're also sending signals about what kind of person you are through your eyes; your facial expression; your body movement; your vocal pitch, tone, volume, and intensity; your commitment to your message; and your sense of humor.

The receiving person is bombarded with symbols and signals from you that reflect your attitude. Everything you do in relation to other people causes them to make judgments about what you stand for and what your message is. *You are the message.*

Your attitude is as important, or more important, than the words you say to your customers. Consider this example:

> A man who was waiting to board a plane decided to have a soft drink. When he went to the counter to order it, the clerk greeted him with "Yeah," instead of "How may I help you?" The man asked the clerk for a medium soda. The clerk didn't say anything. He just turned around and began preparing the soda. When he was finished, he turned to the customer and said glumly, "That'll be $1.03."

> The traveler paid for the drink, and the clerk said nothing more, not even a simple "thank you." The look on the clerk's face clearly indicated that he didn't want to be behind that counter.

Have you ever been in a similar situation? What did you think about the service you received?

As you can see, attitude plays an important part in customer service.

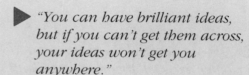

"You can have brilliant ideas, but if you can't get them across, your ideas won't get you anywhere."

Lee Iaccoca

Consider this checklist of attitudinal factors:

✓ *Do you like yourself?* If not, customers likely won't either. Again, remember the words of the late Earl Nightingale: "Attitude is a reflection of self-esteem." People who have low self-esteem usually don't like themselves, their surroundings, or their life. They should concentrate on setting goals to change or, in some instances, seek professional counseling.

✓ *Are you always aware of how you are representing yourself?* Be consistently aware of your voice tone, facial expressions, and other body language.

✓ *Do you genuinely like other people?* If you don't, you probably don't want to be in the field of customer service. More important, consider how you can make yourself more comfortable being around other people. It is a life skill that you need—for social as well as for professional situations.

✓ *Are you eager to help others?* People who don't care keep others waiting. In customer situations, show that you care by being on time every time and by approaching or calling customers in a timely fashion.

✓ *Do you have a positive outlook?* This includes your outlook about your job, your company, and the future. If you have a negative attitude about these things, it will be obvious to the customer. Consider what you must do to change yourself or your environment. However, be aware that your environment usually is not at the core of a negative outlook. More than likely, a negative outlook is the result of an esteem issue or an internal conflict.

✓ *Do you strive to be the best you can be?* In this quality-oriented world, your attitude must be to continually provide the best service you can. Second-rate quality won't get you success. Strive for continuous quality improvement.

▶ *"If you can't get people to listen to you in any other way, tell them it's confidential."*
Farmers Digest

Essential Telephone Skills **for Excellent** *Customer Service*

"One of the surest ways to rub someone wrong is to take too long on the telephone."

George Walther
Telephone communications expert

Common Telephone Complaints

Several studies asking people to list their biggest complaints about telephone usage have turned up these results:

- Slow answering
- Improper or unclear announcements
- Incorrect transfers (the customer is disconnected or given the wrong party)
- Using poor grammar and giving evasive answers
- Leaving the line or being put on hold
- No sales effort (an "I don't care if we make an impression or not" attitude)
- Improper close (An accounting clerk provides data to a salesperson in the company who asked for it. After giving the data to the salesperson, the clerk says, "I hope that's it," instead of "Let me know if I can help further.")

19 Dealing With Telephone Complaints

1. What complaints would you add to the previous list?

_____

_____

_____

_____

_____

_____

_____

_____

_____

_____

2. Now, get together with some of your co-workers and share with them the common telephone complaints listed on page 102, as well as those you added in #1. Then place the items in the proper columns below. For areas where you could improve, brainstorm ideas for improvement.

Areas that are not a problem for our company:	Areas where our company could improve:
_____	_____
_____	_____
_____	_____
_____	_____
_____	_____

The Dos and Don'ts of Telephone Etiquette

Do ...

- **Be businesslike.** You must also be courteous, friendly, and pleasant.
- **Smile into the telephone.** Even though the caller can't see you, he or she can get an idea of what you look like. You can help to create a positive image.
- **Rehearse common scenarios.** Be prepared. Anticipate questions and situations.
- **Enunciate clearly.** Speak slowly enough that the other person understands your message.
- **Be aware of your voice tone.** Because you cannot use nonverbal communication on the telephone, your voice tone and words must convey the message. Over 80 percent of telephone communication is tone of voice.
- **Identify yourself and your department or position,** whether you are receiving a call or calling someone else. This is called *self-disclosure.*
- **Answer all calls within three rings.** Two rings are preferable.
- **Use the caller's name during the conversation.** Lean toward being formal (Mr., Ms., Miss, Mrs.) until the caller indicates that it is okay to use his or her first name. This is particularly true when talking to people from other countries or cultures that tend to be more formal in business communications.
- **Take the time to educate callers about your company's products or services.** Muddling through explanations will not only test your customers' patience but also make them wonder about the reliability and quality of the company in general.
- **Visualize the person you are speaking to.** Try to keep the image positive.
- **Concentrate on the caller's real message** even though he or she may not convey it clearly. Listen intently.

Don't ...

- *Interrupt.* Few things are more likely to anger your customers.
- *Eat or drink anything while you are talking on the phone.* There's nothing worse than hearing someone crunch in your ear or listening to someone with a mouth full of food try to talk.
- *Seem bored or annoyed.* Be aware of your tone of voice.
- *Leave the phone unattended.* If you must be away from your desk, communicate to the person who receives your calls where you will be and when you will return.
- *Argue with customers, no matter how angry you might get.* Keep your emotions in control and monitor your voice tone.
- *Talk to someone beside you while you are on the phone.* This, too, can be very irritating to the caller. Remember, you must concentrate on the customer. That means giving the customer your full attention.
- *Contradict.* Even if your customers are dead wrong (and sometimes they are), explain your point of view with the facts you have available.
- *Give out information at random, particularly if you don't know the customer.* If you give customers the wrong information or make promises the company can't keep, you put your company in a bad position. Likewise, don't give out confidential company information to those who are not authorized to receive it.
- *Lie.* It is unethical. If someone is in a meeting, say so. If someone is not, don't say that he or she is. Tell the caller that the person is unavailable right now.
- *Sound unsure.* Don't guess. Find out.
- *Badger the caller for the reason for the call.* If you are screening calls for someone, ask only once, "May I ask the reason for the call?"
- *Keep a call on hold.* Twenty seconds is the maximum amount of time you should put a person on hold before asking whether the person would like to continue holding.

Staying Organized to Serve Customers Effectively

Consider this scenario: You are on the telephone with a customer who is seeking important information from you—information that was just in front of you. But now it's disappeared. You say to the customer: "Where did that information go? It was just here. I know it's here somewhere. Let me put you on hold while I look for it." Or worse, "Let me call you back when I find it." You have just sent out two messages to the customer:

1. I am wasting your time and mine.
2. I don't know what I'm doing. I am disorganized.

Does this scenario sound familiar? Hopefully not. Use the rating scale that follows to help you determine how your telephone organization rates.

20 Rating Your Telephone Organization

Circle the number that best reflects your skill in each area. "1" indicates "Needs Improvement"; "5" means "I do this well."

	Needs improvement				I do this well
1. Keep clutter off of your desk when talking with customers.	1	2	3	4	5
2. Keep important files that you refer to regularly close to your desk, so that you don't have to put customers on hold while you go to the central files.	1	2	3	4	5

3. Use a long telephone cord or a cordless phone so that you can walk around and be accessible to items you need while talking to customers (using a long cord is possible only if you are not working in close proximity to others).   **1   2   3   4   5**

4. Have a handwritten agenda when you call others so that you can speak to specific concerns and stay focused on key information.   **1   2   3   4   5**

5. Always keep a notepad by your phone to paraphrase customer comments. It's not a good idea to say: "Wait a minute. Let me get something to write on."   **1   2   3   4   5**

6. Understand thoroughly how your phone works. That may sound obvious, but today most phones have many features and high-tech attachments. Many of them need to be programmed. Take time to learn what your phone can do. It's disconcerting to customers to be "cut off" because you push the wrong button.   **1   2   3   4   5**

7. Always keep your calendar in a place where it won't get lost or buried under other papers. Having easy access to your calendar can help you define deadlines and delivery dates with customers. (For best results, you may choose to use a calendar software program on your computer.)   **1   2   3   4   5**

8. Meet with your receptionist or administrative assistant (or if you are one, with your supervisor) to organize your day and to determine which calls must get through. Communicate with each other.   **1   2   3   4   5**

Here are some tips for staying organized:

- ***Keep your desktop neat and clean.*** Have only the paperwork related to what you are doing before you at the moment. How's that for a challenge? This does not mean that you must keep your desk totally cleared off. If you have neat stacks and files related to your other projects on your desk, keep them off to the side or in a file basket. If you don't, here's what will happen: When a customer calls, you take out the file relevant to your discussion. After hanging up with that customer, the phone immediately rings again, before you have time to put the file away from your last conversation. Then a third call comes in, and possibly a fourth. Before you know it, information that you need is buried under other files and you find yourself saying: *"I know it's here somewhere."* This scenario leads to the next point.

- ***Always immediately put away customer files you are not using.*** Do not have a "to be filed" basket or pile. Another name for a "to be filed basket" is "clutter." When you finish speaking with a customer, discipline yourself to file away the information relevant to that customer's call. If another call comes in immediately, move the information or file regarding the last call to the side of the desk. Then, when you have a few minutes between calls, put the unused files away. Avoid creating a stack of "to be filed" material. As the stack gets bigger, you may tend to procrastinate putting it away. Then, if a customer calls, the file will be buried in your "to be filed" basket rather than in your file drawer. Since the files in your basket won't be in alphabetical order, it will take you considerable time to find the information you need. What do you find yourself saying to your customer? *"I know it's here somewhere."* Then you'll have to put your customer on hold or ask if you can call back when you find what you need. What impression do you make on your customers? That you are disorganized and, by transference, that your company is disorganized too.

- ***Keep your customer files in alphabetical order within arm's reach of your telephone.*** This way you can usually locate what you need immediately, without leaving the phone or putting your customer on hold. If you depend on "central files" located outside of your immediate work area, it means that you must leave the phone, put customers on hold, or call them back. Also, since you may not be familiar with the filing system of the central files, which was usually developed by someone else in the company, you are at the mercy of the secretary or file clerk who developed the file system to find what you want. And, of course, if this person is at lunch, on vacation, on a break, or somewhere else, what is the end result? You have a customer who is kept waiting.

- ***Use a cordless phone or a phone with a long cord to facilitate mobility.*** A phone with a long cord allows you to stay on the line with your customer as you seek out customer files or other information, which is better than keeping your customer on hold. And if your work area is already organized, you can stand up and move around to locate key information. You increase your mobility to locate items that may be across the room in a different location. Of course, be practical. Long phone cords can become a hazard if there is a lot of foot traffic in your work area.

- ***Use a good day planning calendar for organization.*** A good day planner has a month-at-a-glance calendar, a daily calendar, and a telephone/address section. Use your day planner to organize your work each day and to list the telephone calls you need to make to customers and to note at what time you will call them.

- ***Make and return calls in chunks of time.*** Define on your day planner when you will call customers. Perhaps you will make phone calls between 9:00 a.m. and 10:30 a.m. and then again between 2:00 p.m. and 4:00 p.m. This will help you to reserve time for follow-through with other customers you have already talked to. Of course, some customer service jobs require a staff person to be available for phone calls most of the day.

- ***Put together a handwritten agenda before calling customers.*** Have a clear idea of what you want to say before calling customers. Organize your thoughts on paper.

Getting Organized on Paper to Serve Customers on the Telephone With Quality

Figure 10 shows an example of how to use an organizer to plan your day and to work in chunks of time to serve customers more efficiently.* Being organized will help you to follow through and live up to the commitments you make to your customers. As you can see, a good day planner provides room for you to jot down a brief agenda next to the name of each person you need to call.

Taking Telephone Messages for Others

Consider the following scenario: Your co-worker's telephone rings. She's not in. Your company doesn't have voice mail. The phone rings four or five times. Other employees who are sitting close to her telephone and walking by pay no attention to the ringing phone. Their attitude is "Hey, it's not my phone."

But guess who's calling?

SOMEBODY'S CUSTOMER!!!

Always answer your phone (and your co-workers' phones if they aren't around) preferably within three rings unless, of course, your company has voice mail.

If you answer a co-worker's phone, take a clear, helpful message. Many commercial message pads do not encourage the message taker to get meaningful information from the customer. A form similar to that illustrated in Figure 11 can be more helpful. Figure 12 provides a full-page form that may be photocopied.

*For more information about using day planning calendars and getting organized, please see Jim Temme's book entitled *Productivity Power: 250 Great Ideas for Being More Productive*, published by SkillPath Publications, Inc.

① Working in these time blocks focuses your commitment to follow through in calling your customers.

② This time block shows how you will follow through on meeting customer requests.

③ It is important to list names of callers and a handwritten agenda about what you want to discuss. This helps to organize your thoughts and prevents you from forgetting key agenda items that you need to discuss with customers.

Weekly Priorities

Send follow-up letters to customers who made purchases last week.

Monday	4-18
Tuesday	4-19
Wednesday	4-20
Thursday	4-21
Friday	4-22
Saturday	4-23
Sunday	4-24

To Do List

To Do

③ Phone Calls...

• *Mary Miller—about her late order*

• *Gene Wilson—about 1) date of delivery for widgets 2) installation 3) discuss warranty*

• *Lisa Denton—about 1) questions regarding her order 2) would she like a free catalog*

⑤
• *Open mail*
• *Write field reports*
• *File customer reports*
• *Learn new product features*

Daily Schedule For _18th_

Monday

7:00	
:30	
8:00	
:30	
9:00	① *Return phone calls to customers*
:30	
10:00	
:30	② *Follow through on customer orders*
11:00	
:30	
12:00	
:30	
1:00	*Cold calls to potential customers*
:30	
2:00	
:30	① *Return calls to customers*
3:00	
:30	
4:00	
:30	
5:00	
:30	*Pick up clothes from cleaners*
6:00	
:30	
7:00	④
:30	*Softball game*
8:00	
:30	

④ Be sure to take care of your personal life to keep your job of serving customers in perspective. Have hobbies and other interests as meaningful outlets for fun and relaxation.

⑤ Identifies other tasks you have on this day.

Figure 10. A good organizer helps you to serve customers more efficiently on the telephone.

1 *Always state the full name of the customer.*

2 *The telephone message should always state the customer's need(s). Then, the employee can research how to fulfill those needs before calling back.*

3 *It is important for the message taker to summarize what was said to the customer. The message taker should be careful not to make comments for co-workers.*

A Telephone Message for You

Jim Temme Phone message for: **Dave Brink**
Message Taker   Name

1 *Bill Holt*   **4** (314) 837-X X X X
Customer's Name   Customer's Phone Number

2 Customer's need: *Mr. Holt was calling about 1) the status of his order—it hasn't arrived yet. He thought he would receive it yesterday: 2) a confirmation on the price.*

5 Customer's demeanor: *He seemed a little bit agitated, but not unpleasant. I don't think he'll be angry if you can call him before the end of the day.*

3 What I told the customer: *That I would give you the message. I told him you were at a meeting until 2:00 p.m. and that you would likely call later today.*

4 *Be sure to get the area code if it is a long-distance call.*

5 *It is helpful to know the attitude or mood of the customer who is calling. Have you ever returned a call to a customer who immediately was belligerent and unpleasant? If you are aware ahead of time that the customer is agitated, you can be better prepared to handle the call.*

Figure 11. Elements of a useful telephone message pad. Take time to serve your internal customers well by taking meaningful messages for them. Remember, everyone who calls your company is somebody's customer.

A Telephone Message for You

_____ Phone message for: _____
Message Taker   Name

_____   _____
Customer's Name   Customer's Phone Number

Customer's need: _____

_____

_____

_____

Customer's demeanor: _____

_____

_____

_____

What I told the customer: _____

_____

_____

_____

_____

Figure 12. Sample telephone message pad.

The Voice Mail Dilemma

Although voice mail is probably here to stay, it does present a dilemma. Many companies are struggling with the question of whether voice mail is customer-friendly. It is a technology that you or your company will want to think through clearly. Before investing in it, you may want to consider voice mail's advantages and disadvantages.

Advantages of Voice Mail

- The phone is always answered.
- The phone can be programmed to ring no more than three times.
- People are now conditioned to leaving messages and will usually do so.
- If customers leave messages, it gives you a chance to prepare an answer to their question or to gather the material you need before you call them back.
- Voice mail is much more professional than answering machines. Background noise is minimized.
- Voice mail allows you to communicate with internal customers without interrupting them.
- Voice mail minimizes personal interruptions.
- Voice mail allows you to work in time blocks. You will more likely be able to pick up your messages at your convenience and return some calls in chunks of time. Of course, some customer service positions do not allow you this convenience.
- You can retrieve your messages from distant locations. If you are traveling, you can still make contact with your customers.
- Voice mail minimizes phone tag.
- You can receive messages from your customers after normal work hours. Likewise, you can leave messages after hours for your customers who have voice mail.

Is Voice Mail an Advantage?

List the advantages that voice mail may offer you and your company.

_____

_____

_____

_____

_____

_____

_____

_____

_____

_____

_____

_____

Disadvantages of Voice Mail

- Customers (particularly external customers) may interpret voice mail as cold and impersonal.
- There is no opportunity for an exchange; therefore, you can't ask questions—there is no opportunity for feedback.
- Some people still refuse to leave messages, but this isn't as much a problem as it used to be.
- Voice mail can become so convenient for internal customers that people stop making the effort to meet with each other face to face.
- Sometimes voice mail can be so convenient that internal customers begin to leave messages that aren't necessary. Then when you check your messages, you find that many of them are irrelevant or meaningless.
- There is little opportunity for you to sell yourself, your products, or the services of your company.
- It can discourage face-to-face contact, particularly between employees or between supervisors and their staff (internal customers).

22 Recognizing the Disadvantages of Voice Mail

What precautions does your company need to take in using voice mail?

_____

_____

_____

_____

_____

_____

_____

_____

_____

_____

_____

_____

Here are some tips for using voice mail:

- *Use a brief, upbeat salutation or greeting.* Remember that over 80 percent of your communication on the telephone is tone of voice. Let callers know that you are pleased they called.

- *Update your message to reflect when you are away from your place of business and when your customers can expect to receive a call back from you.* A word of caution: If your business is in your home, be careful with this idea. When you inform people that you will be away from your home office for an extended period of time, you are issuing an open invitation for someone to rob you.

- *Check your messages on a timely basis.* To a certain extent, how often you check your messages depends on the nature of your job. Some people need to check their messages hourly. For others, daily will suffice. Just be sure to return customer calls promptly. Gather information and respond to their requests quickly and with quality.

- *Use voice mail only as a backup.* Too many people and companies use it as a crutch. If your job is really customer-oriented, take as many calls as feasible rather than depending on and abusing voice mail. Customers want to talk to real people.

- *Before automatically leaving a voice mail message with an internal customer, think first.* It might be better to walk down the hall to your co-worker's desk so that you can deal with the situation in person.

- *Return voice mail messages in chunks of time.* If you are incessant about checking your voice mail messages and returning calls immediately, you may find yourself becoming crisis-oriented. As discussed before, you should always return calls to your customers on a timely basis, but think first. Have you gathered the information the customer needs? Have you thought through what you want to say? In other words, are you being proactive (thinking before acting) and working with quality?

CHAPTER 12

Re-engineering: **Transforming Yourself and** *Your Organization*

"There ain't no rules around here! We're trying to accomplish something."

Thomas Edison

Re-engineering and Quality Customer Service

Remember that customer service is about meeting needs. That means always improving your products, services, procedures, and yourself as an employee. That's what this book has been about—improving yourself, in particular, to provide quality customer service. Remember that quality in customer service is about high attention to follow-through and caring.

Re-engineering is redesigning products, services, procedures, delivery systems, management philosophies and styles, training systems, and

The Old ➡	Re-engineered to ➡	The New
• Fire fighting		• Fire preventing
• Telling employees what to do		• Getting employee input to enhance quality
• Supporting a top-down hierarchy		• Teamwork
• Supporting top-down problem-solving		• Seeking employee input to solve problems (two heads are better than one)
• Focusing on the task and being cost-driven		• Focusing on the customer and being customer-driven
• Recognizing one correct approach		• Recognizing and implementing creative solutions/ continuous improvement
• Shooting from the hip and blaming people when things go wrong		• Gathering data that can help solve real customer problems rather than blaming employees

problem-solving processes to enhance quality and, ultimately, to serve customers more efficiently.

Re-engineering is a process of providing internal customer service by making necessary structural and procedural changes so that employees can serve external customers with greater quality.

Applying Quality Principles to Customer Service

Dr. W. Edwards Deming, whom we have discussed throughout this book, is renowned for his "14 Points" to enhance quality in the workplace. These principles are related to the idea that if you produce quality goods and services, you will keep your customers and earn new ones.

Below is a list of Deming's 14 points, paraphrased and adapted to the process of Total Quality customer service:

1. ***Your company should have a mission statement that reflects its values.*** Among its values should be quality goods and services and meeting customer needs. (See Chapter 5.)

2. ***Adopt the philosophy of continuous quality improvement.*** Quality improvement must be a new way of thinking, not a promotional campaign. Management and employees must consistently "walk the talk."

3. ***Do it right the first time.*** Commit to quality each time you make a product, provide a service, call a customer, prepare a report, attend a meeting, and so forth.

4. ***End the practice of securing materials, products, and services on the basis of price tag alone.*** In other words, be sure that your suppliers and vendors give you quality material and services so that you can meet your customers' needs. Getting the lowest price from them isn't necessarily the lowest price. Think about it.

5. ***Continually improve the delivery system of your goods and services.*** Concentrate on quality, productivity, and reducing costs.

6. ***Provide training and development opportunities for internal customers on an ongoing basis.*** Do staff members have the skills to serve customers efficiently?

7. ***Institute leadership.*** Continuously improve yourself to solve customer problems and to make decisions. Serve yourself to improve yourself so that you can take charge and lead when customer situations call for it. If you are a manager, empower your staff. That's real leadership.

8. ***Drive out fear in the workplace.*** Develop an environment of "job intimacy." This is an environment that allows employees to speak up and to act without fear of retribution. To solve customer problems, to improve procedures and products and services, creativity is needed. For creativity to happen, internal customers must feel comfortable and safe presenting new ideas.

9. ***Break down barriers between departments.*** Departments need to communicate with each other and share information—not compete with each other. Work together to compete against the external competition.

10. ***Eliminate slogans and wild exhortations.*** Walk the talk. Fancy buttons and cute slogans are not customer service. Treating customers humanely and following through to meet their needs is customer service. Remember, customer service is not a promotional campaign. It is a way of life.

11. ***Eliminate quotas.*** Concentrate on meeting customer needs from the start. Always emphasize a quality transaction and relationship rather than define quotas you must live by.

12. ***Consider "pride of skill."*** Take pride in what you do. Be a real professional.

13. ***Institute a vigorous program of education and self-improvement.*** Don't stop learning. School is never out. (See Chapter 3.)

14. ***If you are a supervisor or manager, you set the tone.*** Model positive customer service behavior for your employees. Take care of them. Meet their needs. If you do, your customers will more likely care for your company's external customers.

Re-engineering Requires Change: The Organization and You

Remember that re-engineering is related to making necessary structural and procedural changes in order to serve internal and external customers better. Yet change is not easy for us; we have a tendency to resist it. According to Billy Hodge and Herbert Johnson in their book *Management and Organizational Change,* there are several areas of change where resistance may occur:

- Changes that are perceived to lower status or prestige
- Changes that cause fear
- Changes that affect job content and/or pay
- Changes that reduce authority or the freedom to act
- Changes that disrupt established work routines
- Changes that rearrange formal and informal group relationships
- Changes that are forced without explanation or employees' (or customers') participation
- Changes that are resisted because of mental and/or physical lethargy

In her book *The Change Masters,* Rosabeth Moss Kantner describes "kaleidoscope thinking." She says that when you were young, you may have owned a kaleidoscope. As you turned it gradually, the colors and shapes would change. But do you remember growing impatient and shaking up the kaleidoscope so that the colors and patterns would change drastically? Rosabeth Moss Kantner uses this analogy to suggest that many organizations and companies need to drastically change the way they do business. In customer service, many organizations need to stop running customer service promotional campaigns and begin living out quality customer service day after day. A change in overall behavior may be needed.

In their book *The Feel of the Workplace,* Fritz Steele and Stephen Jenks suggest that there are three components of a successful change strategy:

1. *Choose the right targets for change.* In Total Quality Management and re-engineering, the concept is to continually look at what needs to change to serve customers most efficiently. It doesn't mean

that everything must change at once. Select your target areas for change; that will make the biggest difference to your customers.

2. ***Involve the right people.*** Who needs to be involved in making and implementing the changes? Select internal and external customers who are likely to understand, embrace, and implement the changes.

3. ***Make sure the timing is right.*** Don't try to make too many changes at once. Get people gradually used to change. Don't suggest new changes when your customers are just getting used to the last change.

More Suggestions on Making Changes to Better Serve Customers

If companies (really, people in companies) rest on their laurels, they are moving backwards. Because while they are sitting back, other companies are moving forward—being progressive and implementing new ideas to improve products, services, and procedures. Constantly encouraging change and moving forward should become part of your company's culture.

Here are some more suggestions for making change happen:

- ***Define any changes specifically.*** In other words, know what you want as an end result. Change for the sake of change is wasteful and unproductive.

- ***Anticipate resistance.*** Be prepared to support why a change is necessary. For instance, if it is necessary to change your inventory procedures to improve quality in delivery time for your customers, it may be inconvenient for those who have to implement the change. They may resist.

- ***Explain why the change is necessary.*** This may be the most important point about change. People want to know why they should change and what the benefits will be.

- ***Sell your basic ideas—build coalitions.*** Don't expect people to just accept change. Be prepared to sell the features and benefits of the changes you are asking for.

- ***Involve people in the anticipated change.*** This, too, is very important. If you want commitment, get input and ideas from those who will be directly influenced and affected by the change. Then really listen to what those people are saying. Try to incorporate their ideas into the change.

- ***Praise your internal customers when they implement and succeed.*** Let them know that you appreciate their willingness to change.

- ***Coach employees through mistakes so that they learn.*** Never put people down or use negative feedback when they are trying to make a change. Criticism will only cause them to retreat into their comfort zone. They will then be less likely to embrace change in the future.

- ***Have a good time.*** Change can be fun as well as profitable if you pay attention to these suggestions. Your customers will be the real winners.

13

Self-Management:
Dealing With the
Stress of Providing
Quality Customer Service

*"There is nothing quite so valuable as work.
That's why it's a good idea to leave some for
tomorrow."*

Marian Dolliver

The Stress of Working With Others

Working with other people is usually rewarding, invigorating, and satisfying. However, too much continuous contact with customers, without any relief, can become very stressful. Being on the phone all day long with one customer after another can have an insidious effect. Your frustration and anger can build. Your mood can change. Before you are aware of it, you can start snapping at other people or inadvertently start expressing your bad mood or frustration through your voice tone or body language. We all need an occasional break to collect our thoughts and recharge our batteries.

Contact overload syndrome is the name psychologists have given the phenomenon of dealing with too many people over and over.

Whether or not you experience contact overload syndrome may well be related to the type of job you have. Some jobs require a great deal of customer contact. Others don't.

A job with *high emotional labor* is a job with considerable people contact.

A job with *low emotional labor* is a job with fairly low people contact.

Even if you thoroughly enjoy people, you probably still need your space. And, of course, it's not only the extreme people contact that can be stressful. Other stressors include too many deadlines, lack of prioritization or changing priorities, conflict, rushed meetings, and noncompliant co-workers.

When we feel harried, we tend to be reactive. To be in control is to be proactive.

> *Proactive behavior:* Thinking before acting
> *Reactive behavior:* Acting before thinking

Remaining Calm Under Pressure

Being in control is proactive behavior. Dealing with lots of customers, some of whom are angry, can be upsetting. Likewise, too many phone calls or meetings, too much paperwork, disagreements with internal and external customers, and trying to accomplish too much in too little time can be stressful. A proactive professional learns how to take control and to remain CALM, even under adverse conditions.

Here are some tips for staying cool and calm when you are experiencing contact overload syndrome:

C — *Control the climate*. Talk to yourself positively. Say to yourself that you will be able to handle whatever situation you find yourself in. If others are upset, emotional, and harried, model calm behavior for them. Be in control.

A — The behavioral psychologist Dr. Albert Ellis referred to the precipitating condition (angry customers, too much work, unmet deadlines, changing priorities) as the *activating event*. It is the trigger event that makes you angry and reactionary. Ellis said that we have a tendency to jump to the consequences. Instead, think first.

L — *Listen and think*. If a customer is upset, if there are too many customers to deal with in a short time, if you have too many calls to return or too much to do, listen to your customers or to yourself to figure out the best way to handle the situation. In other words, think before speaking and prepare before acting. Be proactive.

M — *Make a response*. Listen first. Think of what you want to say or how you want to act. Then respond.

Staying in Top Condition to Serve Customers With Quality

Contact overload syndrome can take its toll on you and lead to reactive behavior. Here is some information to help you stay proactive—to be in control of yourself and your emotions.

- *Have a safety valve for your emotions.* The previous discussion provided tips on how to remain calm and in control of yourself. However, what if you suppress your anger and emotions all the time? You are likely to blow up at the wrong time at the wrong person. Express your anger, frustrations, and emotions to your "safety valve"—friends and family you trust. Share your feelings with them, as long as it doesn't become a bad habit.

- *Get plenty of rest.* Don't deprive yourself of sleep. If you are overly tired, you are more likely to say and do irrational things. Know how much sleep you need each night. Most people need between six and eight hours of sleep each night.

- *Learn how to relax.* Yes, relaxing requires practice. Learn to relax your body and your mind. Put worry thoughts out of your mind when you are lying in bed at night. Replace them with pleasant thoughts. Only about 2 percent of what we worry about ever comes to pass. Heed the words of Mark Twain: "I've experienced many terrible things in my life, a few of which have actually happened."

- *Exercise.* It's one of the greatest tension relievers. Aerobic exercise is most helpful. Although "the rules" about what constitutes aerobic exercise are changing, generally it is any kind of continuous exercise that is at least 15 to 20 minutes in duration at least three times a week. Something as simple as a brisk thirty-minute daily walk can help you to cope with life's tensions.

- *Prioritize your work and do only one thing at a time.* People have a tendency to get very stressful when their minds are cluttered and they perceive they have too much to do in too short a period of time. If this happens to you and you are interrupted by customers, you may indirectly voice your frustrations in your tone of voice. If you prioritize, you will learn to work on only one thing at a time and keep your work in perspective. You'll also realize that customer interruptions are not aggravations—they are part of the job.

- ***Keep a sense of humor.*** Laughter is another great tension reliever. See the humor in life's situations. Learn to laugh at yourself a little. Don't take yourself or your situations too seriously. Spend time with friends who like to laugh and joke. It will help to keep difficult customer situations in perspective.

- ***Develop hobbies.*** Have outlets that get your mind off work. They help you to be a well-rounded individual. Hobbies help you to relax and to focus on other aspects of your life.

- ***Eat right.*** If you eat junk food and load up on caffeine throughout the day, you are likely to experience emotional highs and lows throughout the day. The sugar high and caffeine can make you hyper. Then when the "high" wears off, you may feel tired. Also, different types of foods affect people in different ways. For instance, some foods make people feel sluggish or stuffy. Listen to your body's signals. Give it fuel that keeps it energized and emotionally sharp.

- ***Give yourself quiet time each day.*** Have a "hermit spot" where you can go to be completely alone, even if it's for only ten minutes a day. Just sit or lie down and practice deep breathing and relax- ation. Melt your tensions away. You need time to yourself.

- ***Create a mental focus.*** Create specific goals to focus on and strive for. People who know what they want in life feel more in control of their lives. Thus, they are usually less stressful.

> ▶ *"When you are at the end of your rope, tie a knot and hang on."*
>
> Theodore Roosevelt

CHAPTER 14

Total Quality
Customer Service:
A Way of Life

———

*There is less to fear from outside competition
than from inside inefficiency, discourtesy and
bad service.”*

Anonymous

To summarize this book, here are a dozen tips to keep in mind when serving customers. These tips will help you to provide total quality customer service and give you "customer power." Remember that customer service is never-ending. It is a way of life.

1. ***Develop customer-friendly systems.*** Make it easy for your customers to locate and contact you. Be accessible. Keep your procedures simple. Minimize paperwork.

2. ***Never lose sight of your company's values.*** Post your company mission statement where it can be easily seen by internal and external customers. Then be sure that you live out what it says. Remember, actions speak louder than words.

3. ***Continually research your customers.*** Find out what they really want and need. Conduct focus group studies periodically. This, of course, is where you have face-to-face, round-table discussions with customers to solicit their feedback on how they feel about your company, your products and services, and your procedures. This is also their opportunity to make suggestions. In addition, conduct easy-to-complete surveys to solicit vital information about how your customers perceive you.

4. ***Seek knowledge continually.*** Learn, grow, and become more knowledgeable. Remember that knowledge is power. It gives you self-confidence and helps you to develop rapport with customers. Never stop learning. School is never out!

5. ***Create value.*** Remember that when you have transactions with customers, they want value for whatever they have exchanged (money, time, energy). Make them feel pleased when they walk away or hang up the phone. They should feel good about the transaction or exchange and feel that they received value.

6. ***Measure what you do.*** In striving for total quality, it is necessary to measure your progress. If you don't measure progress, you can only guess at it. And guessing can be very inaccurate. Here are some things to measure:
   - An increase or decrease in customers
   - Complaint calls
   - Expediency or response time
   - How customers rate your service

7. ***Balance high-tech with "high touch."*** With the aid of voice mail, fax machines, computers, and other high-tech conveniences, we can perform numerous tasks and activities that we never dreamed of too many years ago. It's easy to fall into the trap of using these conveniences in favor of direct contact with customers. Keep in mind that they are tools, not replacements for the human touch.

8. ***Model customer-friendly behavior.*** Let others know that you are there to serve them. Even with irritable, unfriendly customers, you don't have to act like them. Show them, instead, how you would like them to act.

9. ***Be proactive, not reactive.*** Think before you act. In customer situations, always consider what is the best thing to say and the most reasonable way to act to create a positive environment and a meaningful exchange. If you are reactive, you are likely out of control.

10. ***Be visible.*** Be out where your customers are so you can see and be seen. Provide direction. And listen to their input. Take action to accomplish goals and meet needs.

11. ***Give recognition to yourself and others.*** Let people know you appreciate and value them. Take the time to let them know you care.

12. ***Read this book about every six months.*** Doing so will help you remember the principles of total quality customer service. Then implement and practice these principles.

A Final Reminder

Keep yourself and your work in harmony. Strive to be well-balanced. Work hard and play hard. When you are at work, stay focused on what you do. Remember that the difference between a job and a career is focus or commitment.

When you are at work and dealing with your customers, remember:

- Be responsive.
- Be caring and people-oriented.
- Listen.
- Follow up and follow through.
- Have fun.

▶ Customers

… Are those special VIPs who call
    on the phone.

… Are the most important people
    who will ever be in this office.

… Are not interruptions of our work
    … they are the reasons for it.

… Are individuals with names and
    feelings.

… Are not people I argue with.

… Are the reasons I have a job.

… Are not always right, but they are
    always …

▶ The Customer

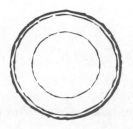

Bibliography and **Suggested** *Reading*

Ailes, Roger. *You Are the Message*. New York: Doubleday, 1988.

Albrecht, Karl. *At America's Service: How Corporations Can Revolutionize the Way They Treat Their Customers*. Homewood, IL: Dow Jones-Irwin, 1985.

Albrecht, Karl, and Ron Zemke. *Service America: Doing Business in the New Economy*. Homewood, IL: Dow Jones-Irwin, 1985.

Bone, Diane. *The Business of Listening: A Practical Guide to Effective Listening*. Los Altos, CA: Crisp Publications, 1988.

Bone, Diane, and Rick Griggs. *Quality at Work: A Personal Guide to Professional Standards*. Los Altos, CA: Crisp Publications, 1989.

Cannie, Joan K. *Keeping Customers for Life*. New York: American Management Association, 1991.

Carlzon, Jan. *Moments of Truth.* New York: Perennial Library, 1989.

Covey, Stephen R. *Principle-Centered Leadership.* New York: Summit Books, 1991.

Finch, Lloyd C. *Telephone Courtesy and Customer Service.* Los Altos, CA: Crisp Publications, 1987.

Gerson, Richard, F. *Beyond Customer Service: Keeping Customers for Life.* Los Alto, CA: Crisp Publications, 1992.

Hanan, Mack, and Peter Karp. *Customer Satisfaction: How to Maximize, Measure, and Market Your Company's "Ultimate Product."* New York: AMACOM, 1989.

Hopkins, Tom. *How to Master the Art of Selling.* Scottsdale, AZ: Champion Press, 1980.

Hodge, Billy, and Herbert Johnson. *Management and Organizational Behavior: A Multidimensional Approach.* New York: Wiley, 1970.

Iacocca, Lee A. *Iacocca: An Autobiography.* Boston: G.K. Hall, 1984.

Kanter, Rosabeth Moss. *The Change Masters: Innovations for Productivity in the American Corporation.* New York: Simon & Schuster, 1983.

Lash, Linda M. *The Complete Guide to Customer Service.* New York: Wiley, 1989.

LeBoeuf, Michael. *How to Win Customers and Keep Them for Life.* Trairie, LA: Michael LeBoeuf and Associates, 1988. Audiocassette

Lickson, Jeffrey E. *The Continuously Improving Self: A Personal Guide to TQM.* Los Altos, CA: Crisp Publications, 1992.

Martin, William B. *Managing Quality Customer Service: A Practical Guide for Establishing A Service Operation.* Los Altos, CA: Crisp Publications, 1989.

Montgomery, Robert L. *Listening Made Easy.* New York: AMACOM, 1981.

Morgan, Rebecca L. *Calming Upset Customers: Staying Effective During Unpleasant Situations.* Los Altos, CA: Crisp Publications, 1989.

Peters, Thomas J., and Robert H. Waterman, Jr. *In Search of Excellence: Lessons From America's Best-Run Companies.* New York: Harper & Row, 1982.

Peters, Thomas J. *Liberation Management.* New York: A.A. Knopf, 1992.

Peters, Thomas J., and Nancy Austin. *A Passion for Excellence: The Leadership Difference.* New York: Random House, 1985.

Sewell, Carl, and Paul D. Brown. *Customers for Life: How to Turn That One-Time Buyer Into a Lifetime Customer.* New York: Doubleday, 1990.

Scott, Dru. *Customer Satisfaction: The Second Half of Your Job.* Los Altos, CA: Crisp Publications, 1988.

Schwartz, David J. *Magic of Thinking Big.* New York: Simon & Schuster, 1987. Audiocassettes

Temme, Jim. *Productivity Power: 250 Great Ideas for Being More Productive.* Mission, KS: SkillPath Publications, 1993.

Walther, George. *Phone Power: Techniques to Communicate Better on the Telephone.* Nightingale-Conant, 1988. Videotape

Walton, Mary. *Deming Management at Work.* New York: Putnam, 1990.

Walton, Sam. *Made in America: My Story.* New York: Doubleday, 1992.